Fortran Programming

Fortran Programming

A complete course in writing Fortran programs

by

JOHN WATTERS

Educational Research Department
International Computers and Tabulators Ltd

HEINEMANN London

Heinemann Educational Books Ltd

LONDON EDINBURGH MELBOURNE AUCKLAND TORONTO
SINGAPORE HONG KONG KUALA LUMPUR
IBADAN NAIROBI JOHANNESBURG
NEW DELHI

ISBN 0 435 77800 5

© International Computers and Tabulators, 1968

First published 1968
Reprinted 1969
Reprinted with corrections 1971
Reprinted 1972

Published by Heinemann Educational Books Ltd
48 Charles Street, London W1X 8AH

Reproduced and printed by photolithography and bound in
Great Britain at The Pitman Press, Bath

Introduction

The American Standards Association (ASA) Fortran, which is equivalent in scope to Fortran IV, has been adopted by most users as their main mathematical programming language.

This text teaches you ASA Fortran using wherever possible complete programs as examples. For these we've used I.C.T. 1900 Fortran which like all implementations of ASA Fortran differs slightly from the original. However when you've completed the text you will have enough confidence to write programs for any machine.

Try to answer all the questions even if at times it seems like hard work. They are mostly in the form of complete programs and will give you experience and provide a useful check on your progress.

Arithmetic Expressions

In ordinary algebra when you write

$$a = x + y$$

you are simply stating that a is equal to the sum of x and y.

In Fortran when we write

$$A = X + Y$$

we are saying: give the variable called A a value equal to the sum of the values of the variables called X and Y. In other words, $A = X + Y$ is not an equation but an instruction to the computer.

A statement such as

$$N = N + 1$$

is meaningless in ordinary algebra but is quite acceptable in Fortran, and has the meaning "Give the variable called N a new value equal to its old value plus one".

The left hand side of an arithmetic instruction in Fortran must contain only the name of a variable. The right hand side may contain any expression whose value we want put into the location named on the left hand side.

QUESTION

State which of the following are unacceptable instructions in Fortran and give your reasons:

$$1. \qquad A = -B$$

$$2. \qquad -B = A$$

$$3. \qquad C = A + B$$

$$4. \quad A + B = C + D$$

$$5. \qquad A = -A$$

Write down your answers before turning over.

ANSWERS

No. 2 is unacceptable.
Signs are not allowed on the L.H.S.

No. 4 is unacceptable.
The L.H.S. contains an expression not a variable name.

Arithmetic Operators

Fortran provides five basic arithmetic operators denoted by the following symbols:

exponentiation **   e.g. $A**2$ means A^2

multiplication *   e.g. $A*B$ means A multiplied by B

division   /   e.g. A/B means A divided by B

addition   +

subtraction   —

There are two simple rules you must observe when writing arithmetic expressions in Fortran:

1. Two operation symbols must not appear next to each other.

$$A* -B$$

must be written

$$-B*A$$

or

$$A*(-B)$$

2. The multiplication symbol must be written where multiplication is intended.

For instance, if you want to multiply A by B you must write $A*B$. If you write AB the computer will assume that you are referring to a single variable called AB.

QUESTION

Write the following expressions in correct Fortran notation, where
A, B and C are variables:

1. $\dfrac{AB}{C}$

2. $\dfrac{A}{-C}$

3. $(A + B)(A - B)$

ANSWERS

1. $A * B \mathbin{/} C$

2. $A \mathbin{/} (-C)$

3. $(A + B) * (A - B)$

When the computer is evaluating an expression it performs all the operations enclosed in brackets first, and evaluates the complete expression in the following way:

1. The sequence of operations is as follows:

exponentiation

multiplication and division

addition and subtraction.

That is, all the exponentiation is performed first, then all multiplication and division and then all addition and subtraction.

Example:

$$A * B * * C \quad \text{means} \quad A \times B^C$$
$$X + 2 * Y \quad \text{means} \quad X + (2 \times Y)$$

2. When the above rules cannot be applied, the expression is evaluated from left to right. You should note particularly the effect of this rule on expressions such as the following:

$$X \,/\, Y * C \quad \text{means} \quad \frac{X}{Y} \times C$$

$$A \,/\, B \,/\, C \quad \text{means} \quad \frac{A}{B \times C}$$

QUESTIONS

Write Fortran expressions corresponding to each of the following expressions:

1. $A + B^4$

2. $(A + B)^4$

3. $A + \dfrac{B}{-C}$

4. $\dfrac{A + B}{C}$

5. $A + \dfrac{B}{C + D}$

6. $\left(\dfrac{A + B}{C + D}\right)^2 + X^2$

7. $\left(\dfrac{X}{Y}\right)^{A - 1}$

8. $\dfrac{\dfrac{A}{B} - 1}{-G \times \left(\dfrac{G}{D} - 1\right)}$

ANSWERS

1. $A + B ** 4$
2. $(A + B) ** 4$
3. $A + B \,/\, (-C)$
4. $(A + B) \,/\, C$
5. $A + B \,/\, (C + D)$
6. $((A + B) \,/\, (C + D)) ** 2 + X ** 2$
7. $(X \,/\, Y) ** (A - 1)$
8. $(A \,/\, B - 1) \,/\, ((-G) * (G \,/\, D - 1))$

Integer and Real Numbers

In 1900 Fortran an INTEGER number is any whole number in the range

$$-8388608 \quad \text{to} \quad 8388607$$

and is held exactly in the computer.

In 1900 Fortran a REAL number is any number in the approximate range

$$-5{\cdot}6 \times 10^{76} \quad \text{to} \quad 5{\cdot}6 \times 10^{76}$$

and is held in floating point form to an accuracy of 11 significant figures.

Constants and Variables

In the statement

$$A = 3 \cdot 4 + B$$

3·4 is known as a CONSTANT.

A and B are known as VARIABLES.

Both Constants and Variables can be of either INTEGER or REAL mode.

Integer Constants

A constant is regarded as being of INTEGER MODE if it is a whole number written without a decimal point or an exponent.

It may be signed or unsigned. If no sign appears it is assumed to be positive.

No commas may appear in an Integer Constant.

For example:

$$8,388,607$$

must be written simply as

$$8388607$$

Real Constants

A constant is regarded as being of REAL MODE if it is a Real number, assumed positive if unsigned and written in one of the following ways:

1. With a decimal point, which may be positioned at the beginning or the end of a number or between two digits.

    For example:

    $$183\cdot$$

    $$9\cdot6$$

    $$\cdot403$$

    are all REAL numbers.

2. With or without a decimal point and followed by an exponent, introduced by the letter E with a one or two digit, positive or negative, power of ten.

    For example:

$53E + 2$	meaning	53×10^2
$\cdot23E - 3$	meaning	$0\cdot23 \times 10^{-3}$
$-4\cdot1E - 5$	meaning	$-4\cdot1 \times 10^{-5}$

    are all REAL numbers.

QUESTIONS

1. Write 1,153

    a) as an Integer number

    b) as a Real number.

2. The following number is written as a Real number with an exponent

$$\cdot153E - 2$$

How would this be written as a decimal fraction?

ANSWERS

1. *a*) 1153

   b) 1153·0 or 1153.

2. 0·00153

Integer and Real Variables

Variables with names beginning with the letters

$$I \quad \text{to} \quad N$$

are regarded as being of INTEGER MODE.

Variables with names beginning with the letters

$$A \quad \text{to} \quad H \quad \text{or} \quad O \quad \text{to} \quad Z$$

are regarded as being of REAL MODE.

Real Mode Arithmetic

When the computer is using Real Mode arithmetic it automatically handles the decimal point, so most of your programming will be in Real Mode.

As you know, most fractions do not have an exact decimal equivalent and similarly neither do they have an exact binary representation. For instance, if the decimal representation of 1/3 to eleven significant figures is added to itself three times, the answer is

·99999999999   not   1·00000000000

and a computer performing this operation would not arrive at the answer 1 exactly.

For most purposes this lack of accuracy does not matter, but you should remember this effect as it can be important in some problems.

Integer Mode Arithmetic

All arithmetic operations on Integers lead to Integer answers. Any results involving fractions are truncated towards zero.

For example:

9/5 would give the result 1 not 1·8

—9/5 would give the result —1 not —1·8

The following Integer expressions are mathematically identical:

$$I/J * K \quad \text{and} \quad I * K/J$$

Let us assign values to each of the variables and see what happens, bearing in mind that in Fortran, calculations are carried out from left to right.

$$I = 14, \quad J = 5, \quad K = 10$$

$I/J * K$ becomes $14/5 * 10$
which becomes $\quad 2 * 10$
which becomes $\quad 20$

$I * K/J$ becomes $14 * 10/5$
which becomes $\quad 140/5$
which becomes $\quad 28$

QUESTION

Evaluate the following expression using Integer arithmetic:

$$2 * I/J + 7/K$$

where

$$I = 13$$
$$J = 5$$
$$K = 3$$

ANSWER

The value of the expression is 7.

Mixed Mode Arithmetic

Real and Integer quantities can be mixed within an expression.

As we have seen, an arithmetic expression is evaluated step by step according to the rules given on page 9.

The mode of each term of an expression depends on the mode of its constituent elements.

If all the constituents of a term are Integer then the term is treated as an Integer sub expression and its mode is Integer. Otherwise any Integer constituent is converted to Real form and the term treated as a Real term.

Example

If A, B and C are Real variables and I, J and K are Integer variables, the expression $A \times B + C/(I + J) - I/K$ would be evaluated as follows:

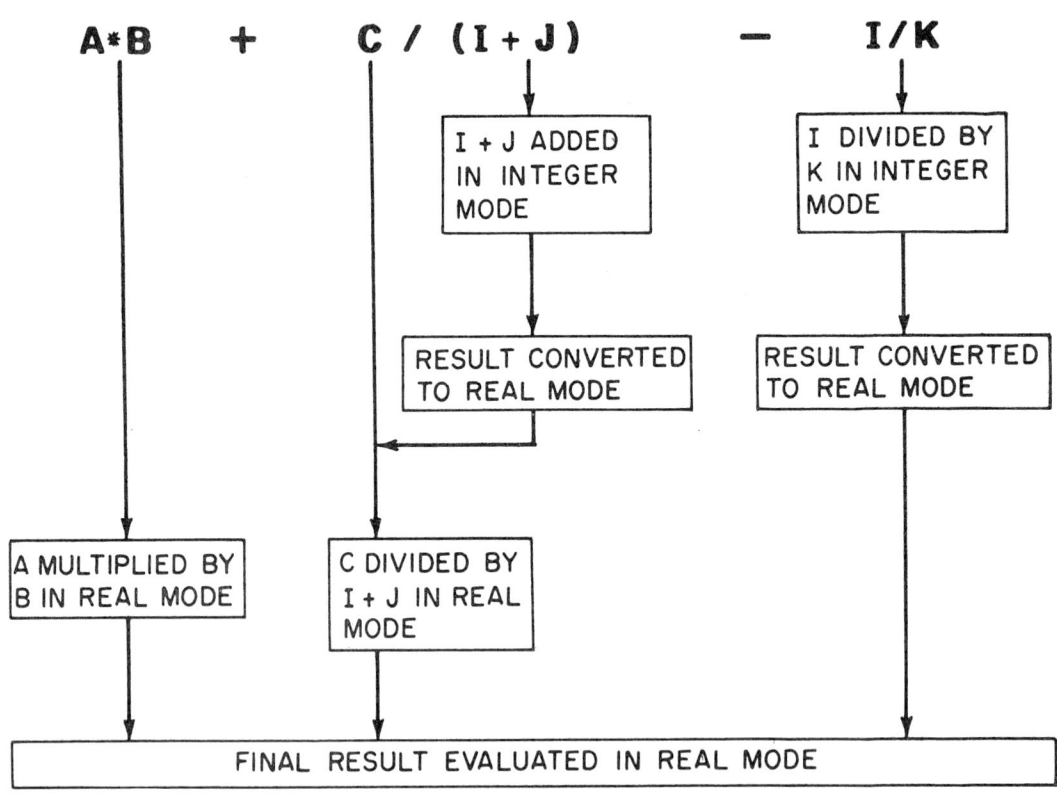

QUESTION

Show the mode of evaluation of the expression

$$A \,/\, (I + J \,/\, 3) + K \times 3 \times J$$

where A is a Real variable and I, J and K are Integer variables.

ANSWER

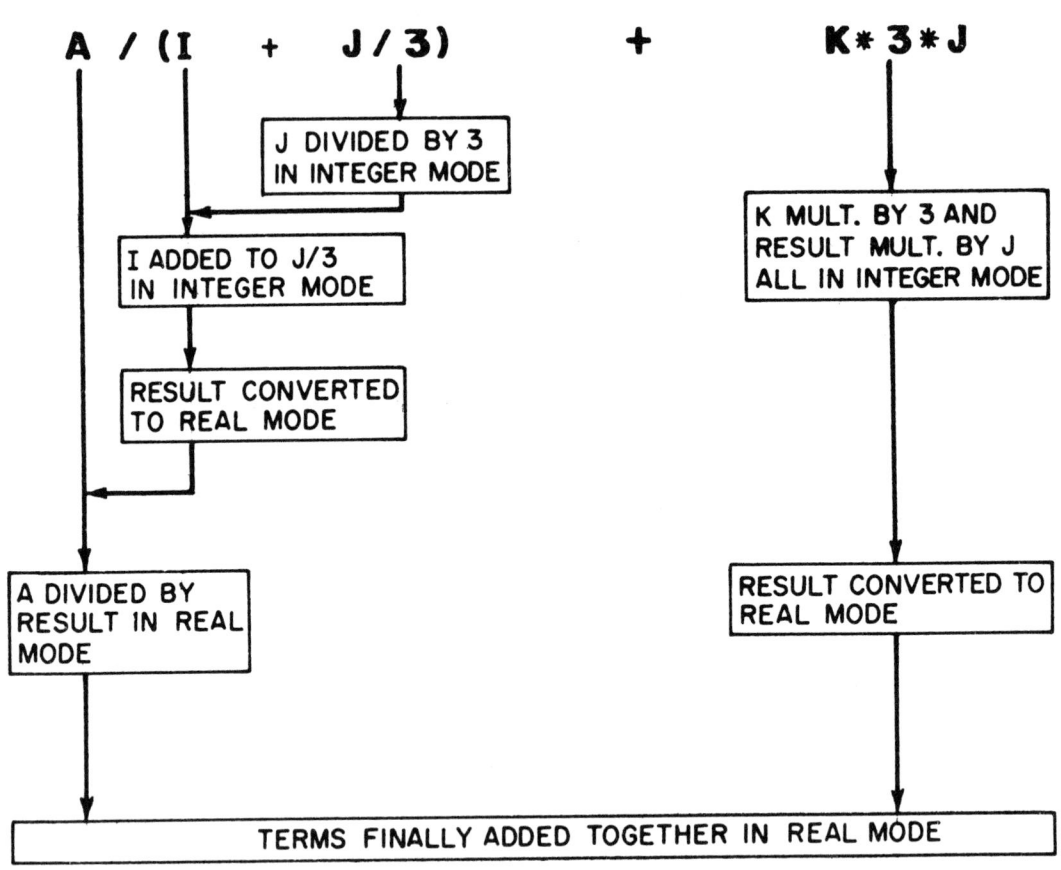

Exponentiation

If *A* and *B* are Real variables and *I* and *J* are Integer variables then:—

I * * **J**   will be evaluated in INTEGER mode.

I * * **A**   *I* will be converted to REAL mode.
The expression will then be evaluated in REAL mode.

A * * **I**   *I* will be converted to REAL mode.
The expression will then be evaluated in REAL mode.

A * * **B**   will be evaluated in REAL mode.

A negative base must not be raised to a Real exponent.

Real and Integer quantities can be mixed in a statement.
If an arithmetic statement is considered to have the form

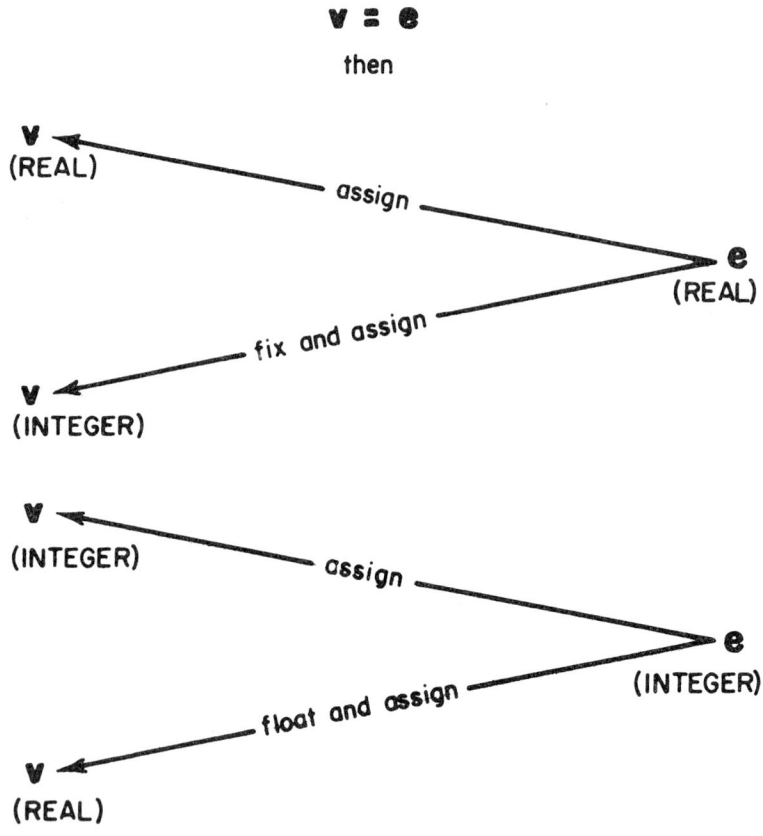

v ≃ e

then

v
(REAL)

assign

e
(REAL)

fix and assign

v
(INTEGER)

v
(INTEGER)

assign

e
(INTEGER)

float and assign

v
(REAL)

Assign means transmit the value without change.
Fix means truncate a Real value to Integer.
Float means convert an Integer value to Real.

QUESTIONS

Calculate the value of the variable on the left if

$$A = 4 \cdot 0, \quad B = -6 \cdot 0, \quad L = 11$$
$$J = 5, \quad K = 2$$

1. $X = A * B - L/J$

2. $X = J/K - B ** 2$

3. $M = B * K - J/3 + 2 \cdot 5$

ANSWERS

1. $X = -26 \cdot 0$

2. $X = -34 \cdot 0$

3. $M = -10$

Standard Functions

Fortran allows you to use certain common mathematical functions, such as sin, cos and tan, simply by writing the correct expression in your program.

For example, if you required the cosine of an angle you would write

$$COS$$

and then IN BRACKETS the angle in radians.

$$COS(X)$$

The arguments of functions are always enclosed in brackets.

In the above example the argument of the function was the single value 'X' but the argument may be any expression within the definition of the function.

For example, you may write:

$$P = W * TAN\ (T + A)$$

Indeed, the expression may contain other functions. For example:

$$P = W * TAN\ (T + A\ /\ COS\ (B\ /\ 2))$$

When using Standard Functions you must ensure that the argument is within the definition of the function.

For example.

If you wanted tan $(J + 2)$ where $J+2$ was an Integer expression you must write

$$\text{TAN (FLOAT } (J + 2))$$

A list of Standard Functions is given in Appendix A.

QUESTION

Write down the following statements in Fortran notation:

1. $R = \sqrt{(A + B)^2 + (C + D)^2}$

2. $C = \cos^2 R - \sin 2 R$

3. $W = \dfrac{RV}{S} \times \log_e \dfrac{V}{X}$

4. $Z = \sqrt{\dfrac{X}{3} \tan 3J}$

ANSWERS

1. $R = SQRT((A + B)**2 + (C + D)**2)$

2. $C = COS(R)**2 - SIN(2*R)$

3. $W = R*V/S*ALOG(V/X)$

4. $Z = SQRT(ABS(X/3*TAN(FLOAT(3*J))))$

Variables

So far when referring to variables we have used only single letters but a variable name can be any string of up to 32 letters and digits.

The first character of a name must be a letter.

Typical variable names are:

MASS   *X*   TEMP1   TEMP2   Z3

Variable names may be chosen to suggest the significance of the variable but the computer will attach no significance to the meaning of the word.

The names of STANDARD FUNCTIONS should not be used as variable names.

Type Statements

As we have seen:—

Variables with names beginning with the letters

$$I \quad \text{to} \quad N$$

will automatically be regarded as being of Integer Mode unless you declare otherwise.

Variables with names beginning with the letters

$$A \quad \text{to} \quad H \qquad \text{or} \qquad O \quad \text{to} \quad Z$$

will automatically be regarded as being of Real Mode unless you declare otherwise.

The mode of a variable may be declared by using a Type Statement:

INTEGER   TIME, CASE, X

REAL   MASS, LINK, ZONE

Without the above statements TIME, CASE and X would be regarded as Real variables, MASS and LINK would be regarded as Integer variables.

The variable ZONE would be treated as Real even if it were not in the Type Statement, but it does no harm to include it.

QUESTION

The following are to be treated as Integer variables:

VAL, TOT, KAY, GOLD, I

NORM, SUMP, LASER

Some of them will be automatically treated as Integers.
Write the Type Statement for those which won't.

ANSWER

INTEGER   VAL, TOT, GOLD, SUMP

Peripheral Units

The data which is associated with a program is punched onto paper tape or cards and is input to the computer by the appropriate peripheral unit, a paper tape reader or a card reader.

The output generated by a program can be recorded in a variety of media. If the output is required by the computer for further processing it will be recorded on paper tape or punched cards by the paper tape punch or the card punch.

If the output is for human consumption the results will be printed out by the line printer.

Each type of peripheral unit is known by a two letter code.

CR	Card Reader
CP	Card Punch
LP	Line Printer
TR	Paper Tape Reader
TP	Paper Tape Punch

So if a program required two card readers, 3 paper tape punches and a line printer the list would be

CR0, CR1, TP0, TP1, TP2, LP0

Units of a particular type are numbered from zero upwards. For example, TP0, TP1, TP2.

QUESTION

What would the list be if in a program you required 3 Paper Tape Readers, 2 Paper Tape Punches and a Line Printer.

ANSWER

TR0, TR1, TR2, TP0, TP1, LP0

Compilation

Programs written in languages such as Fortran are unacceptable to the computer as they stand since the computer can only act on instructions given in its own special code.

The Fortran program is called the source program. A special program known as a compiler is used to translate the source program into the machine's own code. This process of translation is called compilation and is illustrated diagrammatically on the next page.

Compilation

Compilation

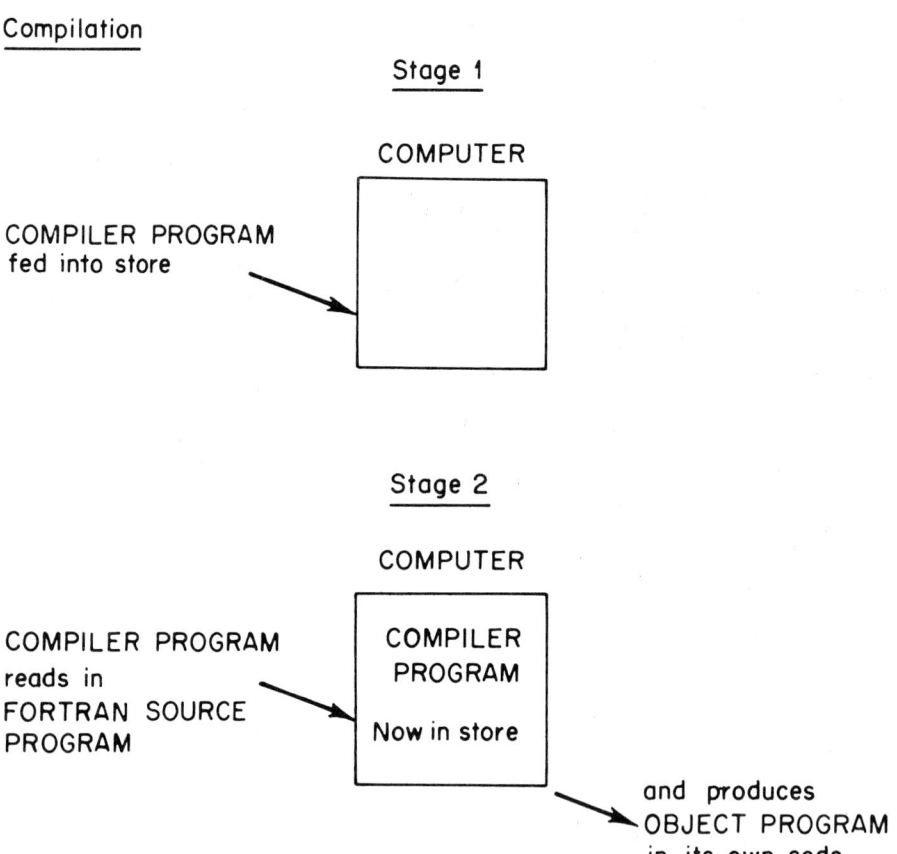

Stage 1

COMPUTER

COMPILER PROGRAM
fed into store

Stage 2

COMPUTER

COMPILER
PROGRAM

Now in store

COMPILER PROGRAM
reads in
FORTRAN SOURCE
PROGRAM

and produces
OBJECT PROGRAM
in its own code

Executable and Non Executable Statements

There are two kinds of statement used in Fortran.

1. Executable Statements.

   These statements are translated by the compiler into the object program.

2. Non Executable Statements.

   These statements are instructions to the compiler. They are not translated into the object program but give the compiler information about the size of the program, the number and type of peripheral units required, the mode of variables, etc.

All Arithmetic Statements are executable statements.

The Type Statements which declare the mode of variables are examples of non executable statements.

The Fortran Coding Sheet

The statements of a Fortran program are written on the standard FORTRAN CODING SHEET. The program is then transferred to some medium acceptable to the computer, either as punched cards or paper tape.

Take great care when writing your programs; a comma missed out or a bracket left unclosed will cause the computer to stop and show an error when compiling your program.

To help the punch room operators distinguish between certain similar characters, the following convention has been generally adopted for use on coding sheets.

Number	Letter
1	I
0	θ
2	$\mathbb{Z}$

For example:

C	STATEMENT NUMBER	CONT.	FORTRAN STATEMENT
1 2 3 4 5	6	7 8 9 10 11 12 13 14 15 16 17 18 19 20 21 22 23 24 25 26 27 28 29 30 31 32 33 34 35 36 37 38 39 40 41 42 43 44	
		INTEGER ZERO, VI1, VI2	
		REAL ØVAL, INPTI, JØBØ	

Capital letters must be used at all times.

A full list of characters available in Fortran is given in Appendix B and you are restricted to these in your programs. Greek letters, for instance, are unacceptable.

Columns 7 to 72 of the coding sheet are reserved for writing program statements.

Each statement must be written on a new line. Spaces in statements are normally ignored by the computer and can be freely used to improve legibility by indenting lines, leaving blank lines and separating symbols and names.

For example:

C	STATEMENT NUMBER	CONT	FORTRAN STATEMENT
1 2 3 4 5	6	7 8 9 10 11 12 13 14 15 16 17 18 19 20 21 22 23 24 25 26 27 28 29 30 31 32 33 34 35 36 37 38 39 40 41 42 43 44	
		REAL I1, I2	
		I1 = I2 * E ** (U + T)	

Columns 73 to 80 are ignored by the Fortran compiler and can be used by the programmer to give the lines of coding sequence numbers.

50

Statement Numbers

Some statements in a Fortran program require labelling with a Statement Number. A statement number can be any number from 1 to 99999 and is written anywhere in columns 1 to 5 of the coding sheet.

No particular significance is attached to the order or size of the statement numbers; they simply provide a means of labelling.

For example:

C	STATEMENT NUMBER	CONT.	FORTRAN
1 2 3 4 5	6	7 8 9 10 11 12 13 14 15 16 17 18 19 20 21 22 23 24 25 26 27 28 29 30 31 32 33 34 35 36 37 38	
1034		DELTA = B * C * SIN(X)	
91		A = SQRT(B*B + C*C)	
3		SUM = U*T - Y**2	

Now let us look at a complete program.

This program computes the Section Modulus of a shaft;

where Z (the section modulus) $= \dfrac{\pi}{32} \left(\dfrac{D^4 - d^4}{D} \right)$

and D (the outside dia) $= 4$

  d (the inside dia) $= 2$

Build up the program on a coding sheet as we go along.

Program Segments

In 1900 Fortran all programs consist of at least two segments.

These are a Program Description Segment and a Master Segment.

For the moment all the programs we shall write will consist of only these two segments.

The Program Description Segment

When you write a program for a 1900 series computer you must begin with the Program Description Segment.

The main use of this segment is to give the program a name and to describe the peripheral units it uses.

The Program Statement

The first thing we do is to give the program a name.

The program name must have exactly four characters. As with every other name in Fortran the first character of the name must be a letter and the complete name must consist of only letters and digits.

Since the program name is used by the computer to identify a particular program the first letter of the name has no mode significance.

This is the first program we shall write, so let's call it EXO1

C	STATEMENT NUMBER	CONT.		FORTRAN
1 2 3 4 5	6	7 8 9 10 11 12 13 14 15 16 17 18 19 20 21 22 23 24 25 26 27 28 29 30 31 32 33 34 35 36 37 38		
		PROGRAM (EXO1)		

Note that the program name is in brackets.

The Output Statement

In this program we shall require a line printer to print out the results.

The Output Statement is used to give a description of the output peripherals required by the program.

The programmer labels each peripheral unit required, with a number which can be any number between 1 and 4095.

Throughout this text the line printer is given the number 60

1	2	3	4	5	6	7	8	9	10	11	12	13	14	15	16	17	18	19	20	21	22	23	24	25	26	27	28	29	30	31	32	33	34	35	36	37	
						P	R	O	G	R	A	M		(	E	X	O	1	)																		
						O	U	T	P	U	T		6	0																						

and to complete the Output Statement we make OUTPUT 60 equal the code word for a Line Printer.

1	2	3	4	5	6	7	8	9	10	11	12	13	14	15	16	17	18	19	20	21	22	23	24	25	26	27	28	29	30	31	32	33	34	35	36	37	
						P	R	O	G	R	A	M		(	E	X	O	1	)																		
						O	U	T	P	U	T		6	0		=		L	P	O																

The End Statement

Every segment in a Fortran program must have an End Statement so the last thing we write in this segment is—END.

C	STATEMENT NUMBER	CONT.		FORTR
1 2 3 4 5	6	7 8 9 10 11 12 13 14 15 16 17 18 19 20 21 22 23 24 25 26 27 28 29 30 31 32 33 34 35 36 37		
		PROGRAM (EX01)		
		OUTPUT 60 = LPO		
		END		

When the program is being compiled the End Statement tells the computer that it has reached the end of a segment.

The Master Statement

Every program must have a MASTER segment:

C	STATEMENT NUMBER	CONT.	FORTR/
1 2 3 4 5	6	7 8 9 10 11 12 13 14 15 16 17 18 19 20 21 22 23 24 25 26 27 28 29 30 31 32 33 34 35 36 37 3		
	MASTER		

We must give the Master Segment a name. You can choose any name you like subject to the same rules as variable names, except that no mode significance is attached to the initial letter. Let's call ours SECMOD.

C	STATEMENT NUMBER	CONT.	FORTRAI
1 2 3 4 5	6	7 8 9 10 11 12 13 14 15 16 17 18 19 20 21 22 23 24 25 26 27 28 29 30 31 32 33 34 35 36 37 38		
	MASTER SECMOD		

58

Since this program is going to be used only once we shall assign the variable values using Arithmetic Statements.

C	STATEMENT NUMBER	CONT.		FOR1
1 2 3 4 5	6	7 8 9 10 11 12 13 14 15 16 17 18 19 20 21 22 23 24 25 26 27 28 29 30 31 32 33 34 35 36 3	
		MASTER SECMOD	
		DMAX = 4.0	
		DMIN = 2.0	
		PI = 3.14159	

Before turning over, write on your coding sheet the Arithmetic Statement needed to compute Z

$$\text{from } Z = \frac{\pi}{32}\left(\frac{D^4 - d^4}{D}\right)$$

ANSWER

ENTER	CONT.	FORTRAN STATEMENT
5	6	7 8 9 10 11 12 13 14 15 16 17 18 19 20 21 22 23 24 25 26 27 28 29 30 31 32 33 34 35 36 37 38 39 40 41 42 43 44 45 46
		MASTER SECMOD
		DMAX = 4.0
		DMIN = 2.0
		PI = 3.14159
		Z = PI/32.0 * (DMAX **4 - DMIN **4)/DMAX

60

Output Statements

We now want the line printer to print out the results in the form shown below:

OUTSIDE DIA	INSIDE DIA	SECTION MOD
4·0000	2·0000	5·8890

Each line of print on the output document is called a RECORD.

The maximum number of character positions in one record depends on the model of line printer. Let's assume that our printer has 121 print positions. The first print position is always left blank. It is reserved for a special paper control character.

Each record can be divided up into one or more FIELDS containing items of data

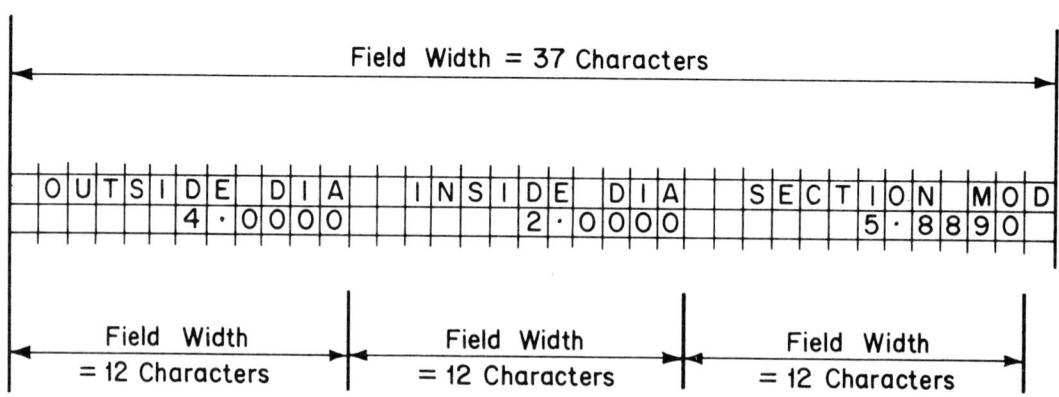

The Format Specification

The FORMAT STATEMENT is a non-executable statement used to supply the computer with a description of each record.

It gives the number of characters in the FIELDS and the form the data takes.

The Format Statement is labelled with a statement number as it is referred to by other statements in the program.

The Format Statement may appear anywhere in the segment in which it is used.

The H Format Specification

The H Format is used to output data in character form.

Since the field width of the heading is 37 characters, the Format Specification will be 37H followed by the characters, including spaces, to be output.

The characters and spacing must be written on the coding sheet in the exact form to be output.

C	STATEMENT NUMBER	CONT	FORTRAN STATEMENT
			MASTER SECMOD
			DMAX = 4.0
			DMIN = 2.0
			PI = 3.14159
			Z = PI/32.0 * (DMAX **4 - DMIN **4)/DMAX
	61		FORMAT(37H OUTSIDE DIA INSIDE DIA SECTION MOD)

This is the only place in any Fortran Statement where spaces in the Statement are not ignored.

64

The Write Statement

The WRITE STATEMENT causes a line of print to be output.

It describes the peripheral unit and the Format which are to be used. It refers to the peripheral unit by the number assigned to it by the programmer. (The number we assigned to the line printer in this program is 60.) It refers to the Format by the statement number of the relevant Format Statement; so to print out the heading we write:

C	STATEMENT NUMBER				CONT	FORTRAN STATEMENT
						MASTER SECMOD
						DMAX = 4.0
						DMIN = 2.0
						PI = 3.14159
						Z = PI/32.0 * (DMAX **4 - DMIN **4)/DMAX
	6	1				FORMAT(37H OUTSIDE DIA INSIDE DIA SECTION MOD)
						WRITE (60 , 61)

The F Format Specification

In the second line of print we want to print out the values of DMAX, DMIN and Z with 4 decimal places.

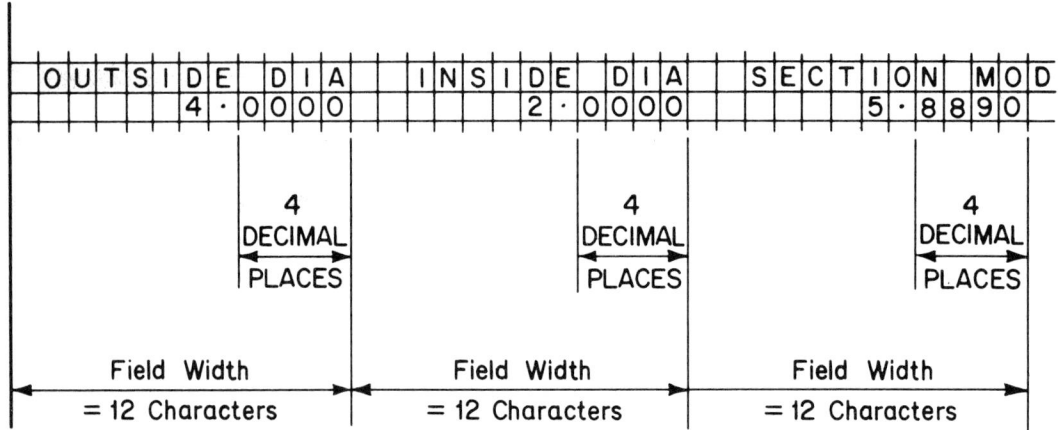

We use the F Format Specification when we want to output Real numbers without an exponent.

The Format Specification for the second line of print is

$$F\ 12 \cdot 4, \qquad F\ 12 \cdot 4, \qquad F\ 12 \cdot 4$$

This will print out the numbers in a field of 12 characters and with 4 decimal places. It automatically prints the number as far to the right in the field as possible.

Since the 3 variables we want printed out all have the same format we can conveniently write: 3 F 12·4

C	STATEMENT NUMBER	CONT	FORTRAN STATEMENT
			MASTER SECMOD
			DMAX = 4·0
			DMIN = 2·0
			PI = 3·14159
			Z = PI/32·0 * (DMAX **4 - DMIN **4)/DMAX
	61		FORMAT(37H OUTSIDE DIA INSIDE DIA SECTION MOD)
			WRITE (60 , 61)
	62		FORMAT (3F12·4)

67

Each Write Statement causes a new record to be output. That is, it automatically prints on a new line.

So the Write Statement for the second line of print is

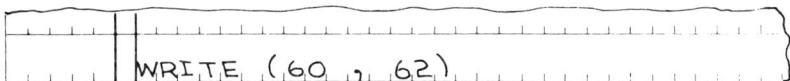

only this time we must list the variables we want output in the order in which they are to be printed. So the full Write Statement is

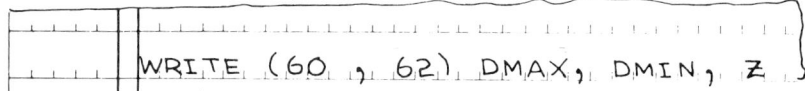

The Stop Statement

The Stop Statement should be the last executable statement of the program.

When the running program reaches the statement

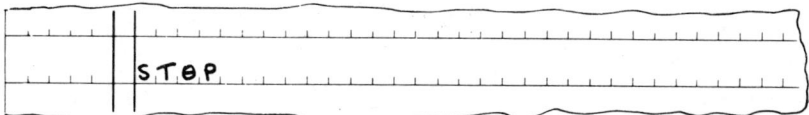

it is deleted from the computer and the program cannot then be restarted.

Since this is the end of a segment, what do you think the next statement in the program will be?

Write your answer on your coding sheet before turning over.

ANSWER

Each segment of a program must have an END STATEMENT, so
the next thing we write is

E N D

The Finish Statement

Each complete program must close with a FINISH STATEMENT. So the last thing we write in this (and in any other) program is

FINISH

Write this on your coding sheet.

When a program is being compiled the Finish Statement tells the computer that it has reached the end of a complete program.

Here is the complete Master Segment.

C	STATEMENT NUMBER	CONT	FORTRAN STATEMENT
			MASTER SECMOD
			DMAX = 4.0
			DMIN = 2.0
			PI = 3.14159
			Z = PI/32.0 * (DMAX **4 - DMIN **4) /DMAX
	61		FORMAT (37H OUTSIDE DIA INSIDE DIA SECTION MOD)
			WRITE (60, 61)
	62		FORMAT (3F12.4)
			WRITE (60, 62) DMAX, DMIN, Z
			STOP
			END
			FINISH

72

QUESTION

Write a complete program to calculate the air standard efficiency of a constant pressure cycle for 2 values of pressure ratio:

$$\text{where } ASE = 1 - \frac{1}{PR^{\left(\frac{G-1}{G}\right)}}$$

where PR1 = 5·5
and   PR2 = 10·5
and   G = 1·4

and print out the following:

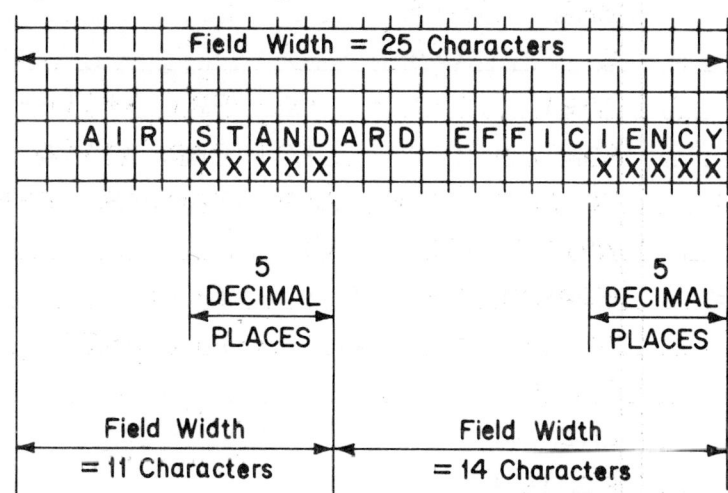

ANSWER

1	2	3	4	5	6	7 8 9 10 11 12 13 14 15 16 17 18 19 20 21 22 23 2
						PROGRAM (EX02)
						OUTPUT 60 = LPO
						END

C	STATEMENT NUMBER	CONT.	FORTRAN STATEME
1 2 3 4 5		6	7 8 9 10 11 12 13 14 15 16 17 18 19 20 21 22 23 24 25 26 27 28 29 30 31 32 33 34 35 36 37 38 39 40 41 42 4
		MASTER AIR
		PR1 = 5.5
		PR2 = 10.5
		G = 1.4
		ASE1 = 1.0 - 1.0/ PR1 **((G-1)/G)
		ASE2 = 1.0 - 1.0/ PR2 **((G-1)/G)
61		FORMAT (25H AIR STANDARD EFFICIENCY)
		WRITE (60 , 61)
62		FORMAT (F11.5 , F14.5)
		WRITE (60 , 62) ASE1, ASE2
		STOP
		END
		FINISH

74

The Input Statement

In the previous example the input data was supplied to the computer in the form of arithmetic statements.

More often programs are designed so that they can be used to solve the same problem with as many sets of data as are required. To do this the input data is put on to punched cards or paper tape and supplied to the computer by a card reader or a paper tape reader.

Fortunately, as we shall see, feeding data into the computer is analogous to recording the results.

EXAMPLE

Let's say we are writing a program to calculate Young's Modulus of Elasticity for a certain material

$$\text{where } YME = \frac{\text{LOAD} \times \text{LENGTH}}{\text{AREA} \times \text{EXT.}}$$

The input data is on a punched card and we want the answer printed out on the Line Printer.

Two peripherals are required by this program, a Card Reader and a Line Printer.

The Input Statement is used in exactly the same way as the Output except, of course, that it describes Input Peripherals.

Try writing the complete Program Description Segment before turning over.

C	STATEMENT NUMBER	CONT.	1 2 3 4 5 6 7 8 9 10 11 12 13 14 15 16 17 18 19 20 21 22 23 24 25 26
			PROGRAM (EX03)
			INPUT 50 = CRO
			OUTPUT 60 = LPO
			END

It doesn't matter if the labels you have chosen for the peripherals differ from the ones shown, but for convenience these labels will be used throughout this text.

Since we want LOAD and LENGTH to be Real variables and their initial letters would cause them to be regarded as Integer, we shall have to declare their mode by using a Type Statement.

Call the Master Segment STEEL and write the required Type Statement on your coding sheet before turning over.

ANSWER

C	STATEMENT NUMBER	CONT.	
1 2 3 4 5	6	7 8 9 10 11 12 13 14 15 16 17 18 19 20 21 22 23 24 25 26 27 28 29 30 31 32 33
		MASTER STEEL
		REAL LOAD , LENGTH

Write the Format and Write statements necessary to print out the first line of the output document in the following manner:

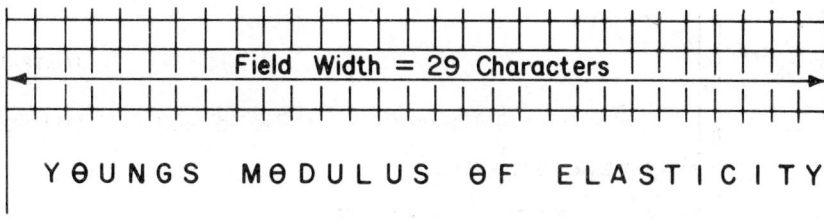

Field Width = 29 Characters

YOUNGS MODULUS OF ELASTICITY

ANSWER

C	STATEMENT NUMBER	CONT.	FORTRAN STATEMENT
			MASTER STEEL
			REAL LOAD , LENGTH
	61		FORMAT (29H YOUNGS MODULUS OF ELASTICITY)
			WRITE (60 , 61)

The Read Statement

The values of the input variables are punched on a card.

A punched card is a record and may consist of one or more fields in the same way as a line of print. A card can hold up to 80 characters.

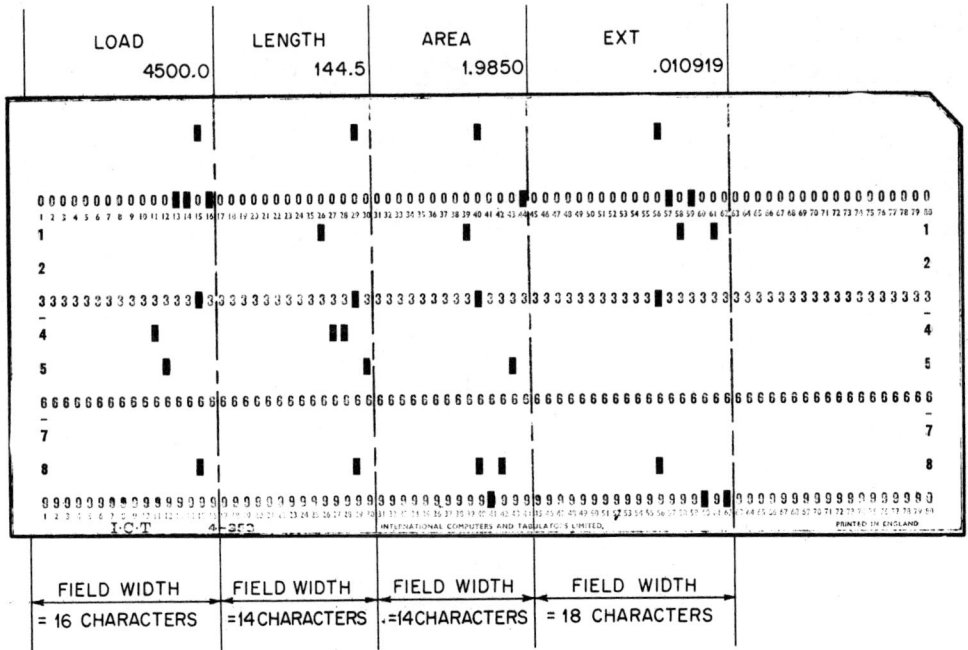

The Read Statement is used to input data and is used in the same manner as the Write Statement.

Write on a separate coding sheet the Format and Read Statements to input the variables.

ANSWER

```
51      FORMAT (F16.1, F14.1, F14.4, F18.6)
        READ (50, 51) LOAD, LENGTH, AREA, EXT
```

Free Format Input

Although the Format Statement shown is perfectly acceptable, we could have written

```
51        FORMAT (4F0.0)
          READ (50 , 51) LOAD, LENGTH, AREA, EXT
```

This is known as Free Format input and can be used for input whenever the following conditions are satisfied:

I Each variable must be separated by at least one space if they are on cards or by a new line character if they are on paper tape.

II If the variable has a fractional part the decimal point must be explicitly punched.

When the variables are being read in, spaces, blank cards or new lines are taken as the end of the field.

ONE WORD OF WARNING!

Don't mix F0·0 format and any other type in the same statement.

Write the Format and Read Statements shown over on your coding sheet.

ANSWER

C	STATEMENT NUMBER	CONT.	FORTRAN STATEMENT
1 2 3 4 5	6	7 8 9 10 11 12 13 14 15 16 17 18 19 20 21 22 23 24 25 26 27 28 29 30 31 32 33 34 35 36 37 38 39 40 41 42 43 44 45 46	
		MASTER STEEL	
		REAL LOAD , LENGTH	
61		FORMAT (29H YOUNGS MODULUS OF ELASTICITY)	
		WRITE (60 , 61)	
51		FORMAT (4F0·0)	
		READ (50 , 51) LOAD, LENGTH, AREA, EXT	

Now write the Arithmetic Statement to compute *YME* from

$$YME = \frac{\text{LOAD} \times \text{LENGTH}}{\text{AREA} \times \text{EXT}}$$

ANSWER

C	STATEMENT NUMBER	CONT	FORTRAN STATEMENT
			MASTER STEEL
			REAL LOAD , LENGTH
61			FORMAT (29H YOUNGS MODULUS OF ELASTICITY)
			WRITE (60 , 61)
51			FORMAT (4F0.0)
			READ (50 , 51) LOAD, LENGTH, AREA, EXT
			YME = LOAD * LENGTH / (AREA * EXT)

Record Separation

After the title we want to leave a blank line before printing the result of the computation.

As we have seen the final right-hand bracket of a Format Statement marks the end of a record.

A slash mark / also marks the end of a record.

If we start the Format Specification for printing *YME* by writing

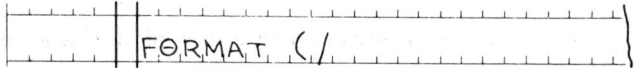

```
        | |FORMAT (/
```

we cause one record to be left blank.

Write this on your coding sheet.

The' same effect could have been achieved by placing the record separation mark at the end of the format for the title

```
FORMAT (29H YOUNGS MODULUS OF ELASTICITY /))
```

Note that a comma is not required before or after the record separation mark.

The E Format Specification

The value of *YME* is to be printed out with an exponent.

The *E* Format Specification causes the number to be printed out as a decimal fraction less than 1·0 but greater than or equal to 0·1 and with an exponent.

If we use the format

$$E\,10\,.\,2$$

the number will be printed out in a field of 10 characters and with 2 decimal places.

The value of *YME* to be output is 30×10^6 and using the format $E\,10\cdot2$ will be output thus:

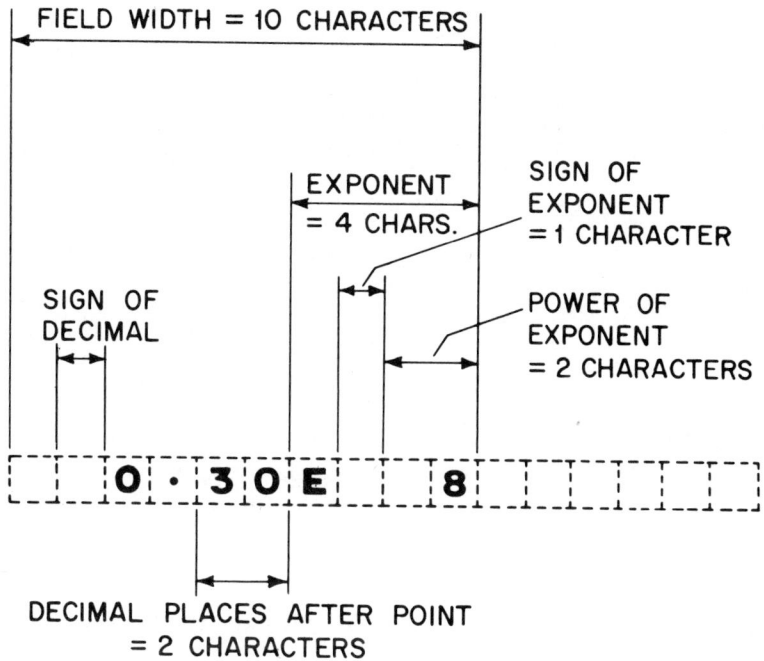

The following points will be noted from the diagram:

I If the sign of either the decimal fraction or the exponent is positive its character position is left blank.

II If the power of the exponent is less than 10 the first character position of the power is left blank.

III As with the *F* Format, the number is printed as far to the right as possible.

Write on your coding sheet the complete Format and Write Statements needed to print out the result in the form:— $0.30E$ 8.

Then write the statements needed to complete the program.

C	STATEMENT NUMBER	CONT.	FORTRAN STATEMENT
			MASTER STEEL
			REAL LOAD , LENGTH
	61		FORMAT (29H YOUNGS MODULUS OF ELASTICITY)
			WRITE (60 , 61)
	51		FORMAT (4F0.0)
			READ (50 , 51) LOAD, LENGTH, AREA, EXT
			YME = LOAD * LENGTH / (AREA * EXT)
	62		FORMAT (/E10.2)
			WRITE (60 , 62) YME
			STOP
			END
			FINISH

QUESTION

We want to write a program to compute the co-efficient of linear expansion of steel from the formula

$$CLEX = \frac{EXP}{LENGTH \times (T2 - T1)}$$

Each item of input data is punched on a card with the decimal point explicitly punched and with spaces between each item.

The input data is punched in the following order:

LENGTH,　　EXP,　　T1,　　T2.

Before turning over try writing the complete program to compute CLEX, printing out the value of CLEX with an exponent and with 4 decimal places after the point.

The output Format Specification shown above gives a field width of 12 character positions. You could use a larger field width but a smaller field would encroach on the first print position which is reserved for the paper control character.

1	2	3	4	5	6	7	8	9	10	11	12	13	14	15	16	17	18	19	20	21	22	23	24	25	26	27	28
						PROGRAM (EX04)																				
						INPUT 50 = CRO																				
						OUTPUT 60 = LPO																				
						END																				

1	2	3	4	5	6	7	8	9	10	11	12	13	14	15	16	17	18	19	20	21	22	23	24	25	26	27	28	29	30	31	32	33	34	35	36	37	38	39	40
						MASTER EXPAN																																
						REAL LENGTH																																
5	1					FORMAT (4F0.0)																																
						READ (50 , 51) LENGTH, EXP, T1, T2																																
						CLEX = EXP /(LENGTH * (T2 - T1))																																
6	1					FORMAT (E12.4)																																
						WRITE (60 , 61) CLEX																																
						STOP																																
						END																																
						FINISH																																

If the variable CLEX had a value of ·00000665, how would it look when printed out?

ANSWER

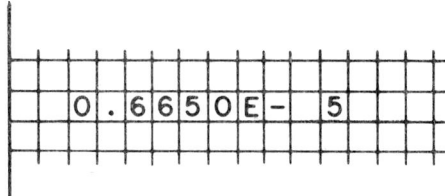

QUESTION

Write a program to compute the volume of a cone from the formula

$$V = \tfrac{1}{3}\pi r^2 h$$

where $\pi = 3.14159$

The radius and height are punched on a card without an exponent. The decimal point is explicitly punched and there is a space between the two variables.

The result is to be printed out in the following manner

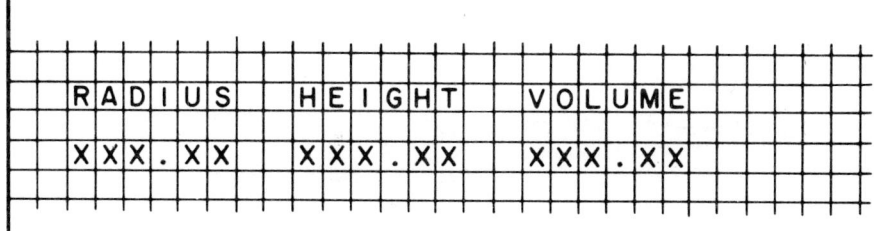

In your program, put the statements to print the heading before those to read in the variables.

97

ANSWER

1	2	3	4	5	6	7	8	9	10	11	12	13	14	15	16	17	18	19	20	21	22	23	24	25	26
						PROGRAM (EX05)																			
						INPUT 50 = CRO																			
						OUTPUT 60 = LPO																			
						END																			

C	STATEMENT NUMBER	CONT.	FORTRAN STATEMENT
			MASTER CONE
	61		FORMAT (24H RADIUS HEIGHT VOLUME /)
			WRITE (60 , 61)
	51		FORMAT (2F0.0)
			READ (50 , 51) RAD, HT
			VOL = 3.14159 * RAD **2 * HT /3.0
	62		FORMAT (3F8.2)
			WRITE (60 , 62) RAD, HT, VOL
			STOP
			END
			FINISH

98

In the program you have just written the computer stops after one set of data has been processed. It is very much the exception to write programs in this way.

Usually the program will be written in such a way that it can deal with as many sets of data as are required.

Let's now look at the ways in which this program can be altered to suit these conditions.

Control Statements

Execution of a Fortran program starts with the first executable statement and thereafter executable statements are taken in the order in which they are written until a specific break in this order is called for.

To allow a jump out of the normal sequence Fortran provides various Control Statements.

The GO TO Statement

In this program we want the computer to go back and read in a fresh set of data after it has printed out the current values of RAD, HT and V∅L.

If we give the Read Statement a Statement Number, say 21, we can write

GO   TO   21

after the Write Statement which prints RAD, HT and V∅L.

C	STATEMENT NUMBER	CONT.	FORTRAN STATEMENT
			MASTER CONE
	61		FORMAT (24H RADIUS HEIGHT VOLUME /)
			WRITE (60 , 61)
	51		FORMAT (2F0·0)
	21		READ (50 , 51) RAD, HT
			V∅L = 3·14159 * RAD **2 * HT/3·0
	62		FORMAT (3F8·2)
			WRITE (60 , 62) RAD, HT, V∅L
			GO TO 21
			STOP
			END
			FINISH

Now when the program is being run each executable statement will be taken in order until the statement

$$GO \qquad TO \qquad 21$$

is reached.

The computer will then return to the statement labelled 21 and repeat all the statements up to GO   TO   21.

```
21    READ (50 , 51) RAD, HT
      VOL = 3·14159 * RAD **2 * HT/3·0
62    FORMAT (3F8·2)
      WRITE (60 , 62) RAD, HT, VOL
      GO TO 21
```

The computer will keep repeating this series of statements indefinitely.

We must now find some way to make the computer leave this loop when there are no sets of input data left.

A common way of stopping a program is to put a dummy card at the end of the input data. On the dummy card we have punched a number, usually a string of 9's or 0's, which we know will not appear on the input data.

Every time data is read in we compare the value of the data with that of the dummy card. When the dummy card is reached we go to the STOP statement.

In this example we shall use a dummy card which has zero as the value of RAD and HT.

The IF Statement

The IF Statement is a control statement which tests if an expression is negative, zero or positive and causes the computer to go to one of three statements depending upon the result.

If we label the STOP Statement, say, 99, we can test for the dummy card by writing:

```
21      READ (50 , 51) RAD , HT
        IF (RAD + HT) 0 , 99 , 0
```

IF (RAD + HT) is negative
    the computer will proceed to the next executable statement (in this case the arithmetic statement to calculate VθL).

IF (RAD + HT) is zero
    the computer will jump to the statement labelled 99 (in this case the Stop Statement).

IF (RAD + HT) is positive
    the computer will proceed to the next executable statement.

The Master Segment now looks like this:

C	STATEMENT NUMBER	CONT	FORTRAN STATEMENT
			MASTER CONE
	61		FORMAT (24H RADIUS HEIGHT VOLUME /)
			WRITE (60 , 61)
	51		FORMAT (2F0.0)
	21		READ (50 , 51) RAD, HT
			IF (RAD + HT) 0, 99, 0
			VOL = 3.14159 * RAD **2 * HT/3.0
	62		FORMAT (3F8.2)
			WRITE (60 , 62) RAD, HT, VOL
			GO TO 21
	99		STOP
			END
			FINISH

QUESTION

What would be the difference in the printed output if, instead of having the record separation mark at the end of the title:—

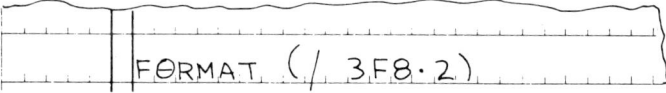

we had put it before the format of the output variables:—

FORMAT (/ 3F8.2)

ANSWER

With the Formats

```
        FORMAT (24H RADIUS  HEIGHT  VOLUME /)
        FORMAT (3F8.2)
```

the output would be:

```
RADIUS     HEIGHT     VOLUME

XXX.XX     XXX.XX     XXX.XX
XXX.XX     XXX.XX     XXX.XX
XXX.XX     XXX.XX     XXX.XX
```

that is a blank record only between the title and the results.

With the Formats

```
        FORMAT (24H RADIUS  HEIGHT  VOLUME)
        FORMAT (/ 3F8.2)
```

the output would be:

```
RADIUS     HEIGHT     VOLUME

XXX.XX     XXX.XX     XXX.XX

XXX.XX     XXX.XX     XXX.XX

XXX.XX     XXX.XX     XXX.XX
```

that is a blank record between each line of print.

108

Flow Charts

Here is a diagrammatic representation of the program we have just done.

This is called a flow chart and is used as an aid in visualising the logic of the problem. Naturally it is done before the program is written.

The flow chart is quite general and each block in the diagram does not necessarily represent only one line in the coding sheet.

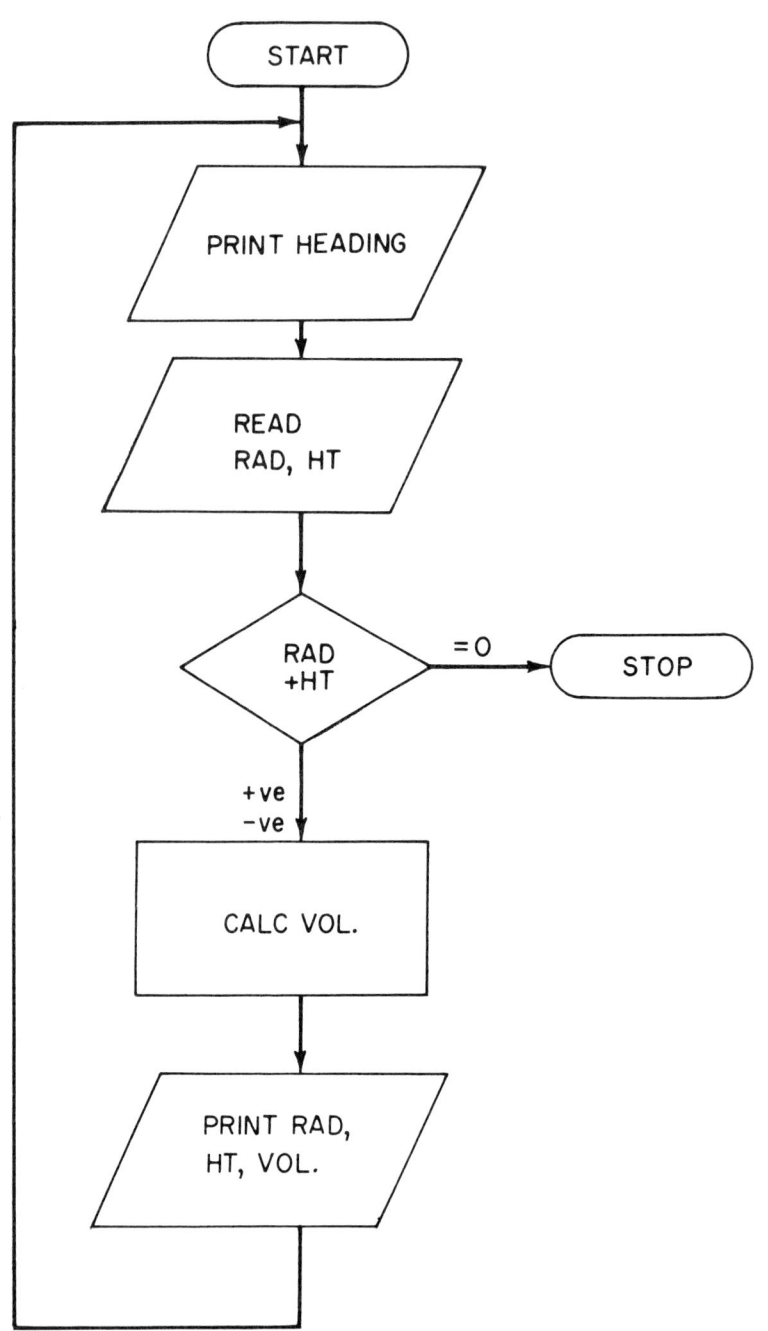

110

You will notice that various shapes of boxes are used in the flow chart. Each shape of box represents a different type of operation.

The generally accepted convention is as follows:

This is the terminal box used to mark the beginning and end of the run.

START

This is the Input/Output box. It's used for any operation which transfers data to or from the peripherals.

READ
RAD, HT

This is the decision box. A good shape because an arrow can lead into one corner and three alternative courses can come from the others.

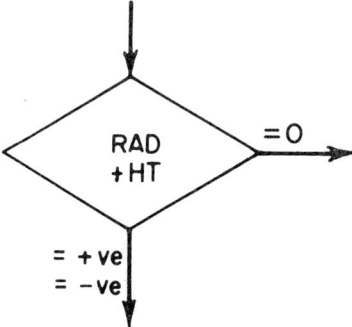

The ordinary rectangular box is used to contain a description of computing operations, e.g. arithmetic operations. A whole series of such operations may be described in the one box as long as they are required in series.

EXAMPLE

The IF Statement has, of course, many more uses than simply testing
for the end of input data.

Here is an example which uses the IF Statement more fully.

The welfare department of a progressive factory wishes to find the
number of workers it employs in each of the following age groups:

A Over the age of 64
   (Workers over the age of 99 are automatically retired on half pay.)

B From the age of 21 to 64 inclusive.

C From the age of 15 to 20 inclusive
   (Workers are encouraged to start their employment with the firm
   at the age of seven, but it is not considered desirable to include this
   age group in the totals.)

The firm wants us to write a program to find the numbers in each age group and has supplied us with the age, in years only, of every worker in the firm.

The data is punched on paper tape with a newline character between each age.

The last record on the tape has the number 100 punched on it.

In programs of this type we must set variables to hold the sums of each age group, call them SUMA, SUMB, and SUMC.

At the start of the program each variable must have a value of zero.

Consider for a moment just one variable.

At the start of the program SUMA = 0

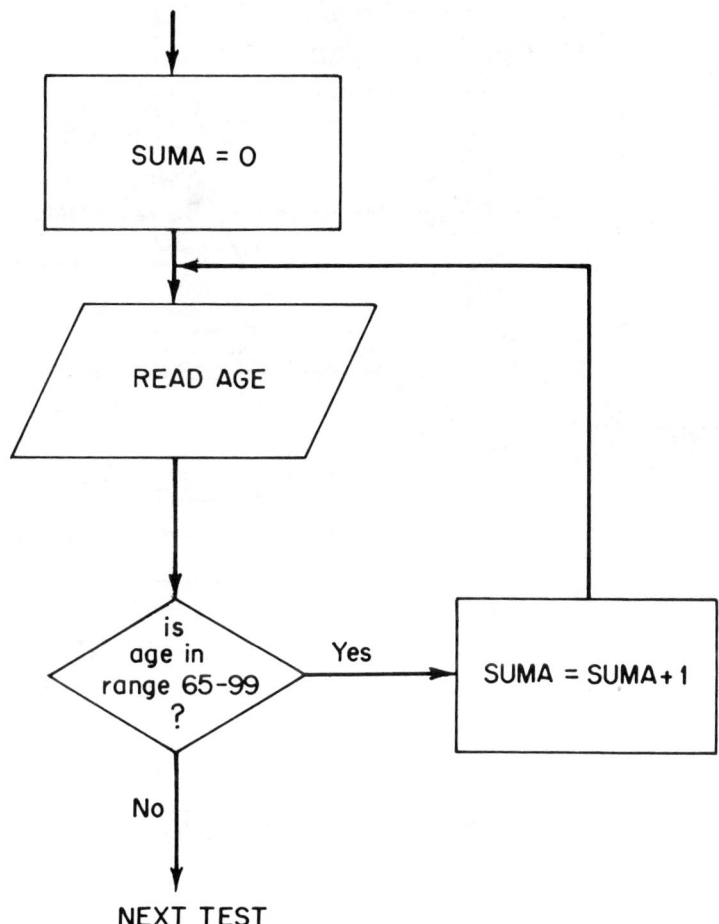

Then each time a number is found to be in the range 65 to 99, SUMA is increased by one.

A typical flow chart for the whole of this problem is shown overleaf.

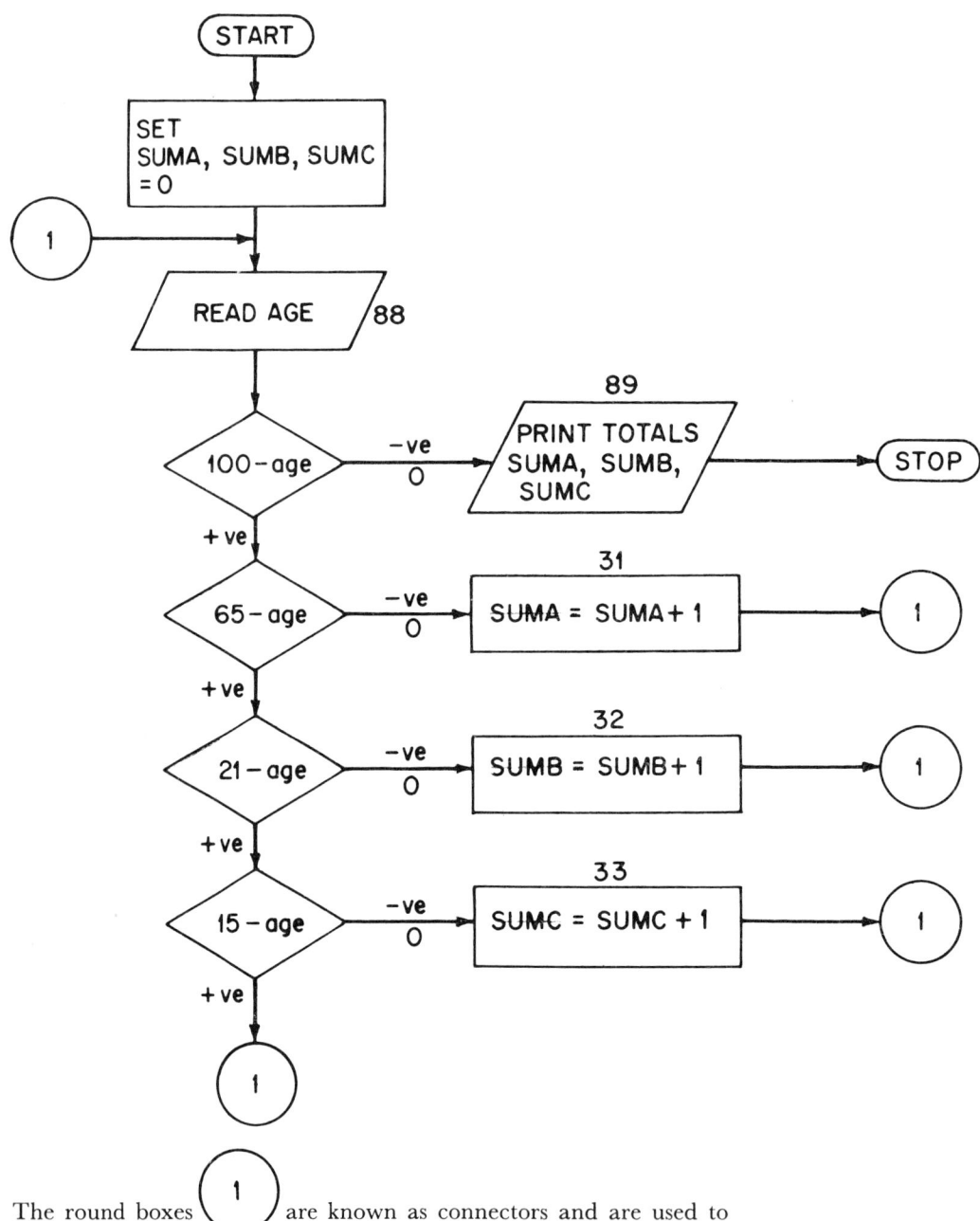

The round boxes (1) are known as connectors and are used to save you drawing connecting lines between the points in the flow chart.

1. Write the Program Description Segment and give the Master Segment a name.

2. Write the Type Statement to declare the variables AGE, SUMA, SUMB and SUMC as being of Integer mode.

ANSWER

1	2	3	4	5	6	7 8 9 10 11 12 13 14 15 16 17 18 19 20 21 22 23 24 25 26 27 28 29 30 31 32 33 34 35
						PROGRAM (EX06)
						INPUT 40 = TRO
						OUTPUT 60 = LPO
						END

1	2	3	4	5	6	7 8 9 10 11 12 13 14 15 16 17 18 19 20 21 22 23 24 25 26 27 28 29 30 31 32 33 34 35
						MASTER WORKER
						INTEGER AGE, SUMA, SUMB, SUMC

118

Multiple Assignment Statement

We must now write the Arithmetic Statement to assign an initial value of zero to SUMA, SUMB and SUMC.

We could do this by writing three separate statements but in 1900 Fortran it is quite valid to use what is known as a Multiple Assignment Statement.

C	STATEMENT NUMBER	CONT.		FO
1 2 3 4 5	6	7 8 9 10 11 12 13 14 15 16 17 18 19 20 21 22 23 24 25 26 27 28 29 30 31 32 33 34 35 36		
		MASTER WORKER		
		INTEGER AGE, SUMA, SUMB, SUMC		
		SUMA, SUMB, SUMC = 0		

The I Format Specification

The *I* Format Specification is used to input and output Integers.

It takes the form *I* followed by the field width.

Since in the example each item of input data is separated by a newline character we can use the Free Format Specification.

C	STATEMENT NUMBER	CONT.	FOR
			MASTER WORKER
			INTEGER AGE, SUMA, SUMB, SUMC
			SUMA, SUMB, SUMC = O
	41		FORMAT (IO)
			READ (40 , 41) AGE

The IF Statement

Here is the general form of the IF Statement.
The IF STATEMENT gives a conditional transfer of control; that is a transfer which depends on a computed result.

It takes the general form

IF (f) nl, n2, n3

where **(f)** may be a single variable or an arithmetic expression.

nl, n2, n3 are Statement Numbers.

IF **(f)** is negative the program jumps to **nl.**
IF **(f)** is zero the program jumps to **n2.**
IF **(f)** is positive the program jumps to **n3.**

Any of the Statement Numbers **nl, n2** or **n3** may be given as 0. If the computed result **(f)** causes transfer to a Statement Number which is 0, the program proceeds with the next executable statement.

Try writing the four IF Statements required in this program, remembering that at the end of the input data we have a dummy record which has 100 punched on it.

Then write the statements needed for incrementing SUMA, SUMB and SUMC.

You can use the numbers written at the side of the boxes on the flow chart as Statement Numbers.

1	2	3	4	5	6	7 8 9 10 11 12 13 14 15 16 17 18 19 20 21 22 23 24 25 26 27 28 29 30 31 32 33 34 35
						MASTER WORKER
						INTEGER AGE, SUMA, SUMB, SUMC
						SUMA, SUMB, SUMC = O
4	1					FORMAT (IO)
8	8					READ (40, 41) AGE
						IF (100 - AGE) 89, 89, 0
						IF (65 - AGE) 31, 31, 0
						IF (21 - AGE) 32, 32, 0
						IF (15 - AGE) 33, 33, 88
3	1					SUMA = SUMA + 1
						GO TO 88
3	2					SUMB = SUMB + 1
						GO TO 88
3	3					SUMC = SUMC + 1
						GO TO 88

Notice that in the last IF Statement IF (15 — AGE) is positive we go back and read in the next variable, since workers under 15 are simply ignored.

124

Output

Write on a separate coding sheet the Format and Write Statements to print out the totals of each age group in a field of 10 characters.

ANSWER

```
61      FORMAT (3 I10)
89      WRITE (60 , 61) SUMA, SUMB, SUMC
```

This is, of course, equivalent to writing

```
61      FORMAT (I10, I10, I10)
89      WRITE (60 , 61) SUMA, SUMB, SUMC
```

With the Format shown above all the variables are printed out on the one line.

In this program we want the variables to be printed on separate lines. We can do this by writing

```
61     FORMAT (I10)
89     WRITE (60 , 61) SUMA, SUMB, SUMC
```

The computer will start a new record when it has printed out one variable but will only stop scanning the Format Statement when the associated list of variables is exhausted.

Write the Format and Write Statements shown and then write the three statements needed to complete the program.

C	STATEMENT NUMBER	CONT.	FORTR
			1 2 3 4 5 6 7 8 9 10 11 12 13 14 15 16 17 18 19 20 21 22 23 24 25 26 27 28 29 30 31 32 33 34 35 36 37

```
            MASTER WORKER
            INTEGER AGE, SUMA, SUMB, SUMC
            SUMA, SUMB, SUMC = 0
41          FORMAT (IO)
88          READ (40, 41) AGE
            IF(100 - AGE) 89, 89, 0
            IF( 65 - AGE) 31, 31, 0
            IF( 21 - AGE) 32, 32, 0
            IF( 15 - AGE) 33, 33, 88
31          SUMA = SUMA + 1
            GO TO 88
32          SUMB = SUMB + 1
            GO TO 88
33          SUMC = SUMC + 1
            GO TO 88
61          FORMAT (I10)
89          WRITE (60, 61) SUMA, SUMB, SUMC
```

FORM 1/542 (8.64)   © Internatonal Computers and Tabulators

| | | | 1 2 3 4 5 6 7 8 9 10 11 12 13 14 15 16 17 18 19 20 21 22 23 24 25 26 27 28 29 30 31 32 33 34 35 36 |

```
            STOP
            END
            FINISH
```

EXAMPLE

Let's construct a program which calculates the roots of a quadratic equation:

$$AX^2 + BX + C = 0$$

from the formula:

$$X = \frac{-B \pm \sqrt{B^2 - 4AC}}{2A}$$

Each set of input data will be on one punched card in a field of 10 characters with 4 decimal places.

At the end of the input data we shall have a dummy card on which A, B and C are all zero.

Start the program by writing the Program Description Segment and giving the Master Segment a name.

ANSWER

C	STATEMENT NUMBER	CONT.																																		
			PROGRAM (EX07)
			INPUT 50 = CRO
			OUTPUT 60 = LPO
			END

C	STATEMENT NUMBER	CONT.																															
			MASTER QUADRAT

The results of the computations are to be printed out as follows:

```
ROOTS   OF   QUADRATIC   EQUATIONS

      A           B           C           X1          X2

   XXX.XX      XXX.XX      XXX.XX      XXX.XX      XXX.XX

                                    ROOTS  COMPLEX
```

131

The X Format

From the form of the output document you can see that in the second line of the heading there are rather a lot of spaces. We could simply write the Format Statement for this line using the H Format Specification and faithfully reproducing the line, spaces and all, on the coding sheet.

Fortunately there is a Format Specification for spaces.

To create space characters on the output document we simply give the number of spaces followed by an X.

We can write the Format Statement for the second line of print as follows:

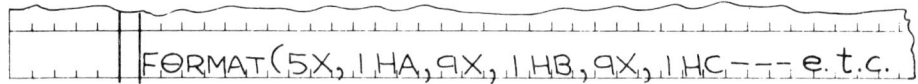

When this line is printed 5 print positions will be left blank before A is printed. A further 9 positions will be left blank before B is printed and so on.

QUESTION

Format Statements can go anywhere in a segment.

So, before turning over, write on your coding sheet the Format Statement for input and the four Format Statements for output.

ANSWER

134

C	STATEMENT NUMBER	CONT.				FORTRAN STATEMENT
			6	7 8 9 10 11 12 13 14 15 16 17 18 19 20 21 22 23...		
				MASTER QUADRAT		
	51			FORMAT (3F10.4)		
	61			FORMAT (11X, 28HROOTS OF QUADRATIC EQUATIONS //)		
	62			FORMAT (5X,1HA,9X,1HB,9X,1HC,9X,2HX1,8X,2HX2 /)		
	63			FORMAT (5F10.4)		
	64			FORMAT (3F10.4, 17H ROOTS COMPLEX)		

Try drawing a flowchart for this program making provision for

$$B^2 - 4AC$$

being negative, zero or positive.

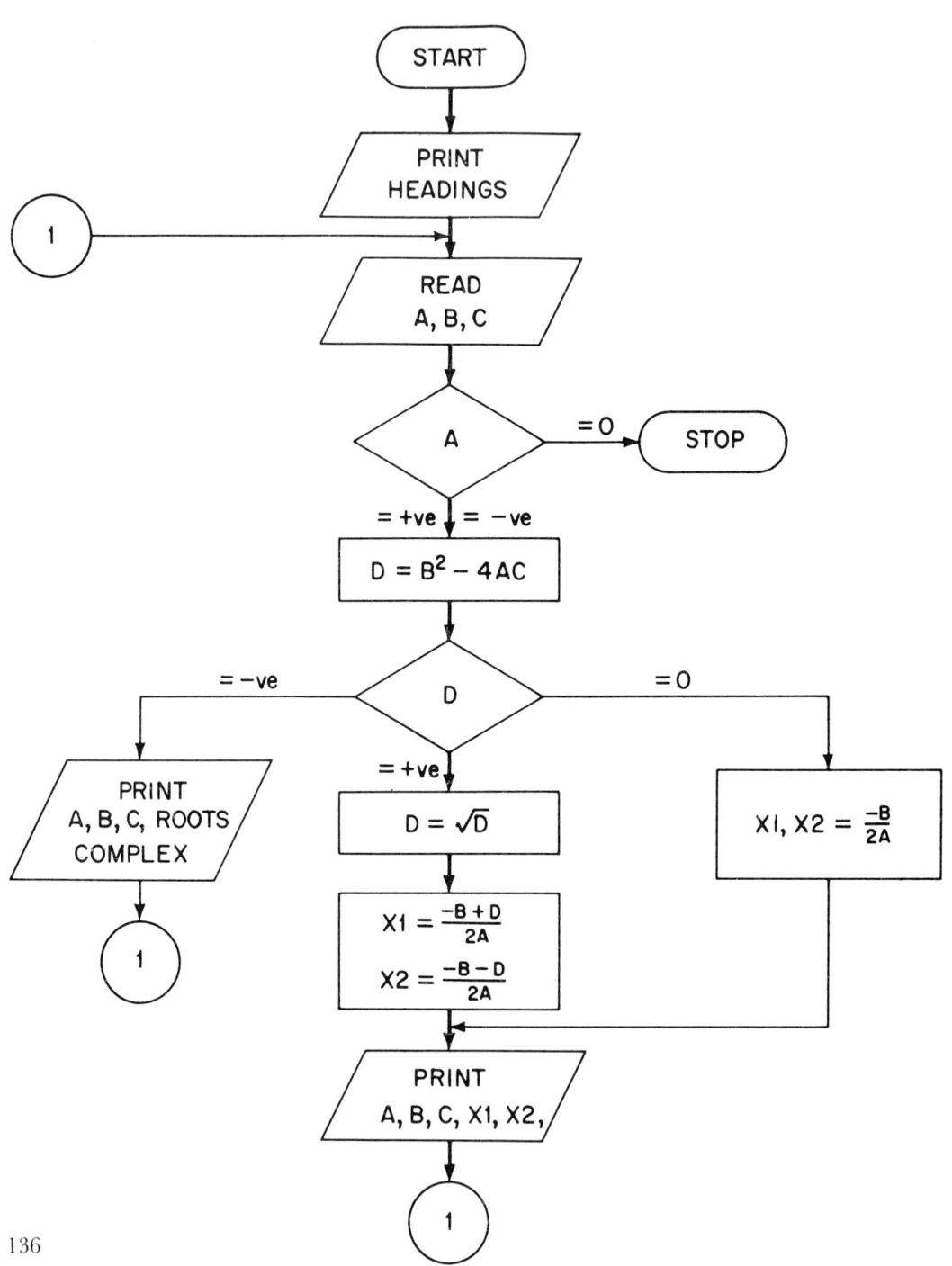

136

Try completing the coding of this program.

Follow the heavy line through first and then do the coding for the loops.

FORTRAN STATEMENT

C	STATEMENT NUMBER	CONT	FORTRAN STATEMENT
			MASTER QUADRAT
	51		FORMAT(3F10.4)
	61		FORMAT(11X,28HROOTS OF QUADRATIC EQUATIONS //)
	62		FORMAT(5X,1HA,9X,1HB,9X,1HC,9X,2HX1,8X,2HX2 /)
	63		FORMAT(5E10.4)
	64		FORMAT(3F10.4,17H ROOTS COMPLEX)
			WRITE (60,61)
			WRITE (60,62)
	89		READ (50,51) A, B, C
			IF (A) 0, 99, 0
			D = B * B - 4 * A * C
			IF (D) 21, 22, 0
			D = SQRT (D)
			X1 = (-B + D)/(2 * A)
			X2 = (-B - D)/(2 * A)
	23		WRITE (60,63) A, B, C, X1, X2
			GO TO 89

Continued opposite

STATEMENT NUMBER	CONT	FORTRAN STATEMENT
22		X1, X2 = -B/(2 * A)
		GO TO 23
21		WRITE (60 , 64) A, B, C
		GO TO 89
99		STOP
		END
		FINISH

139

Iteration

A loop may be an iterative loop in which a calculation is repeated until sufficient accuracy has been achieved according to some criterion; the loop is then left and the program proceeds to the next section.

For example:
Assume that it is necessary in part of a program to calculate e from the series

$$e = 1 + \frac{1}{1!} + \frac{1}{2!} + \frac{1}{3!} + \cdots$$

by direct summation of successive terms up to and including the first term to have a magnitude less than 10^{-8}.

The sum of the first 2 terms is obviously 2 and each subsequent term is derived from the previous one simply by dividing by a counter n.

From the flowchart you can see that at the start of the routine we set E and N equal to 2.

We cannot use a Multiple Assignment Statement for this since in a Multiple Assignment Statement all the variables on the left-hand side must be of the same mode.

Try coding this program from the flowchart.

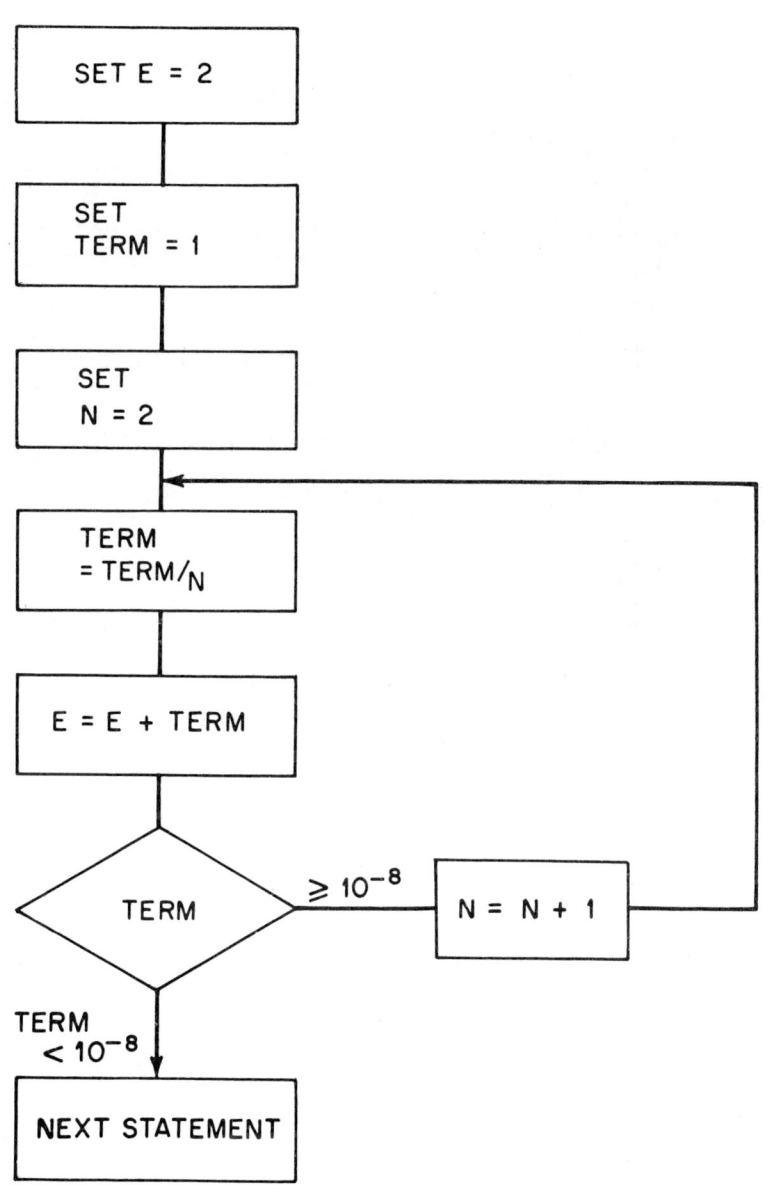

```
          E = 2·0
          TERM = 1·0
          N = 2
21        TERM = TERM / N
          E = E + TERM
          IF (TERM - 1E-8) 22, 0, 0
          N = N + 1
          GO TO 21
22        next statement
```

QUESTION

If the facility were not available in Fortran, it would be possible to calculate $\log(1 + x)$ from the series

$$\log(1 + x) = x - \frac{x^2}{2} + \frac{x^3}{3} - \frac{x^4}{4} + \frac{x^5}{5}, \text{ etc.}$$

where $-1 < x \leqslant 1$.

Draw a flowchart to do this to terms up to and including the first term to have a magnitude of less than 10^{-8}.

Compare the flowchart you draw with the one given over and then write the section of program to compute $\log(1 + x)$.

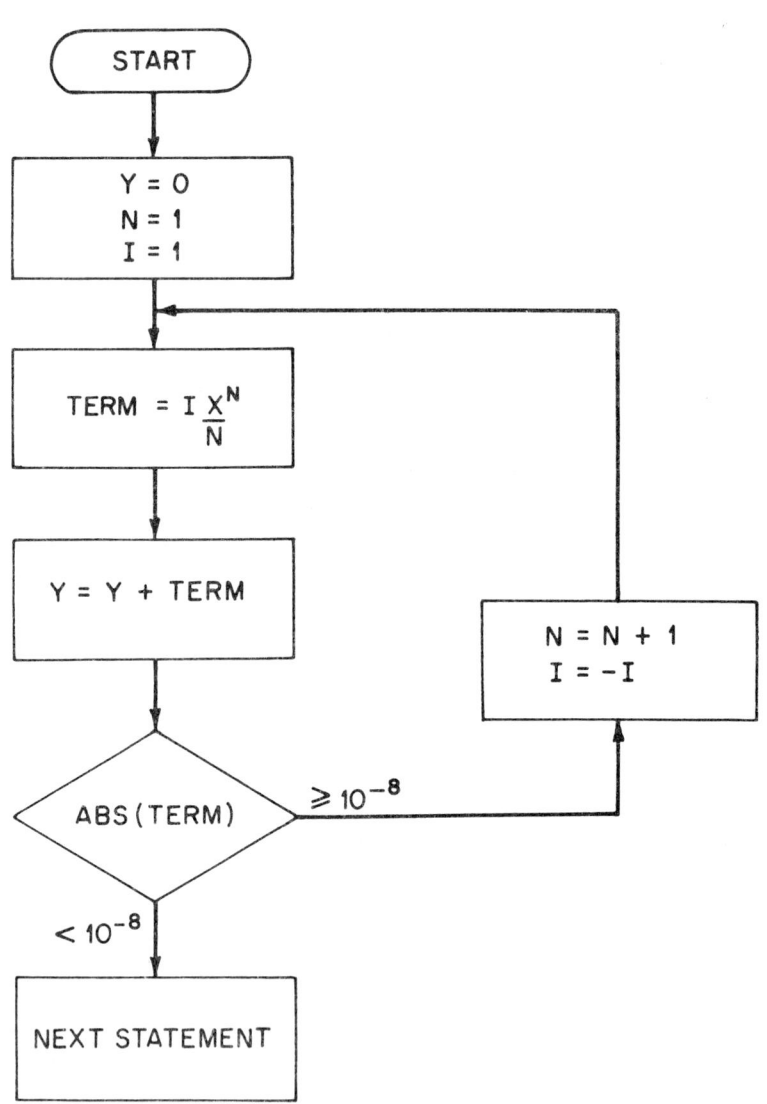

ANSWER

```
         Y = 0.0
         I, N = 1
21       TERM = I * X **N / N
         Y = Y + TERM
         IF (ABS(TERM) - 1E-8) 22, 0, 0
         N = N + 1
         I = -I
         GO TO 21
22       next statement
```

QUESTION

Here is a more difficult problem in iteration you may like to try. (If you'd rather not, feel free to go on to the next section.)

If the facility were not available in Fortran we could calculate $\cos(x)$ from the series

$$\cos(x) = 1 - \frac{x^2}{2!} + \frac{x^4}{4!} - \frac{x^6}{6!} \cdots$$

Draw up a flowchart for this problem to calculate $\cos(x)$. Assume that x has already been calculated. Then write the section of the program needed to calculate $\cos(x)$ up to and including the first term to have a magnitude of less than 10^{-8}.

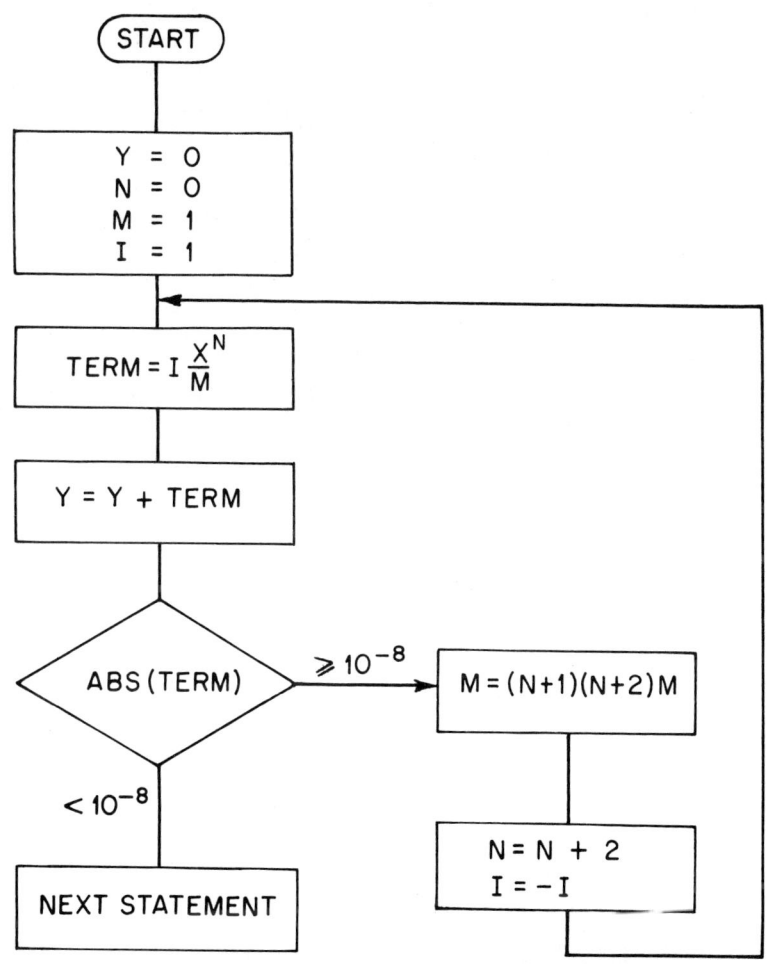

ANSWER

```
          Y = 0.0
          N = 0
          I, M = 1
21        TERM = I * X **N /M
          Y = Y + TERM
          IF (ABS(TERM) - 1E-8) 22, 0, 0
          M = (N + 1) * (N + 2) * M
          N = N + 2
          I = -I
          GO TO 21
22        next statement
```

148

The DO Loop

In the examples we've done which require the control of a loop, we have used the IF and GO TO Statements. Although this is an effective way of controlling a loop, it is rather cumbersome.

Control of a loop by a counter occurs so frequently in programs that Fortran provides a comprehensive statement for this special purpose.

Let's look straight away at a simple example involving the DO loop.

We want to print out the 13 times table.

Here is a program which will calculate the first line of our 13 times
table and print it out thus:

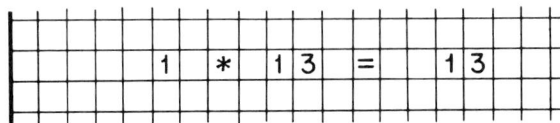

| 1 | * | 1 3 | = | 1 3 |

C	STATEMENT NUMBER	CONT.	
1 2 3 4 5	6	7 8 9 10 11 12 13 14 15 16 17 18 19 20 21 22 23 24 25 26 27 28 29 30 31 32 33
		PROGRAM (EXO8)
		OUTPUT 60 = LPO
		END

C	STATEMENT NUMBER	CONT.	
1 2 3 4 5	6	7 8 9 10 11 12 13 14 15 16 17 18 19 20 21 22 23 24 25 26 27 28 29 30 31 32 3
		MASTER THIRTEEN
		J = 1
		K = J * 13
		WRITE (60, 61) J, K
6 1		FORMAT (I6, 8H * 13 = , I3)
		STOP
		END
		FINISH

150

We want to alter our program so that J takes on every value from 1 to 13.

We want the initial value of J to be one:

$$J = 1$$

We want the final value of J to be 13:

$$J = 1, 13$$

After each product has been computed and printed out we want J to be incremented by one:

$$J = 1, 13, 1$$

If we give the Write Statement a Statement Number, say 33, we can replace the simple statement $J = 1$ by a DO Statement which will give J every integer value from 1 to 13.

$$\text{DO } 33 \; J = 1, 13, 1$$

C	STATEMENT NUMBER	CONT.	
			MASTER THIRTEEN
			DO 33 J = 1, 13, 1
			K = J * 13
	33		WRITE (60, 61) J, K
	61		FORMAT (I6, 8H * 13 = , I3)
			STOP
			END
			FINISH

151

Now, the first time the computer reaches the statement:

$$\text{DO } 33\ J = 1, 13, 1$$

J will be given a value of one.

J will retain the value of one until the computer has executed all the statements following the DO Statement up to and including the statement numbered 33.

The value of J will then be incremented by 1 and the computer will again execute all the statements following the DO Statement up to and including the statement numbered 33.

The computer will continue round the loop, incrementing J by 1 each time, until all the statements have been executed with J having a value of 13.

The DO is then said to be satisfied and the computer will then go on to the next executable statement following the statement numbered 33. In this case it is the Stop Statement.

Let's now look at the general form of the DO Statement.

DO ni = m1, m2, m3

n is the statement number of the last statement of the DO loop. It must, of course, be an executable statement.

The statements following a DO up to and including the one labelled **n** are known as the RANGE of the DO.

i is known as the control variable and must be an Integer variable.

During the execution of a DO loop the control variable **i** is available for any additional purpose permitted for an Integer variable, provided its value is not altered.

If the DO loop is left before it is satisfied the control variable **i** retains its current value.

After a DO loop is satisfied the control variable **i** becomes undefined and nothing can be assumed about its value.

153

m1, m2 and **m3** are known as the indexing parameters. They must all be Integer constants or Integer variables. At the time of execution of the DO Statement all three parameters must be greater than zero.

m1 is the initial value of **i.**

m2 is the final value of **i.**

m3 is the amount by which **i** is incremented after each time round the loop.

When **m3** has a value of 1, it can be omitted from the DO Statement. In this case the preceding comma is also omitted.

For example:

$$\text{DO } 33 \; I = 1, 13, 1$$

is generally written:

$$\text{DO } 33 \; I = 1, 13$$

QUESTION

1. Write the DO Statements which would replace the one given in the example if the table required were:

   a. The thirteen times table up to the product 1300.

   b. If only the even values up to the product 2600 were to be computed and printed out.

2. Write a complete program using a DO loop which will compute the sum of the squares of all the odd integers from 3 to 99. Choose any Format for printing out the result.

ANSWER

1. *a.* DO 33 $I = 1, 100.$
   b. DO 33 $I = 2, 200, 2.$

2.

C	STATEMENT NUMBER	CONT.																												
1 2 3 4 5	6	7 8 9 10 11 12 13 14 15 16 17 18 19 20 21 22 23 24 25 26 27 28 29 30 31 32 33
		PROGRAM (EX09)
		OUTPUT 60 = LPO
		END

C	STATEMENT NUMBER	CONT.																												
1 2 3 4 5	6	7 8 9 10 11 12 13 14 15 16 17 18 19 20 21 22 23 24 25 26 27 28 29 30 31 32 3
		MASTER ODD
		INTEGER SUM
		SUM = 0
		DO 33 I = 3, 99, 2
33		SUM = SUM + I **2
		WRITE (60 , 61) SUM
61		FORMAT (I10)
		STOP
		END
		FINISH

The Continue Statement

The last statement in the range of a DO loop must not be one which causes a transfer of control. For example, none of the following statements should be referred to as the last executable statement:

GO TO

IF

DO

STOP

The Continue Statement is a dummy statement which causes no action to be taken during the running of the program and is used mainly to satisfy the rule given above.

EXAMPLE

If we write the routine to calculate e from the series

$$e = 1 + \frac{1}{1!} + \frac{1}{2!} + \frac{1}{3!} \cdots$$

using a DO loop, we get:

```
        E = 2.0
        TERM = 1.0
        DO 21 N = 2, 20
        TERM = TERM / N
        E = E + TERM
        IF (TERM - 1E-8) 22, 21, 21
21      CONTINUE
22      next statement
```

In this program the loop will be left when a term has been evaluated whose value is less than 10^{-8}.

Rather than work out how many terms are required for the accuracy we want; we simply specify a larger number of loops than necessary, say 20.

This program also illustrates how a DO loop can be left before it is satisfied. The index N will retain the value it had when the loop is left.

158

QUESTION

Rewrite the routine (on page 145) to compute log $(1 + x)$ from the series:

$$\log (1 + x) = x - \frac{x^2}{2} + \frac{x^3}{3} - \frac{x^4}{4} + \ldots$$

using a DO loop.

ANSWER

```
      Y = 0.0
      I = 1
      DO 21 N = 1, 20
      TERM = I * X **N /N
      Y = Y + TERM
      I = -I
      IF (ABS(TERM) - 1E-8) 22, 21, 21
21    CONTINUE
22    next statement
```

Arrays

It is often desirable to represent a set of related quantities by one name and to identify individual values by subscripts. For example, the pressures at various points in a cycle may be referred to as

$$p_1, p_2, p_3, p_4.$$

We can regard p_1, p_2, p_3, p_4 as being a one dimensional array and each individual value as being an array element.

The array shown in the example is written in Fortran notation as

$$P(1), P(2), P(3), P(4)$$

As with simple variables the mode of an array is defined by the initial letter unless a Type Statement is made.

EXAMPLE

To give some idea of the use of arrays in programming, here is an example which computes the mean of a hundred numbers and then computes the standard deviation,

where

$$\text{MEAN} = \frac{\Sigma n}{N}$$

$$\text{Standard Deviation} = \sqrt{\frac{\Sigma(\text{MEAN} - n)^2}{N}}$$

The input data is on paper tape and will be read in using free format specification. The results are to be output on a line printer.

Here is the start of the program:

C	STATEMENT NUMBER	CONT.	
			1 2 3 4 5 6 7 8 9 10 11 12 13 14 15 16 17 18 19 20 21 22 23 24 25 26 27 28 29 30 31 32 33
			PROGRAM (EX10)
			INPUT 40 = TRO
			OUTPUT 60 = LPO
			END

C	STATEMENT NUMBER	CONT.	
			1 2 3 4 5 6 7 8 9 10 11 12 13 14 15 16 17 18 19 20 21 22 23 24 25 26 27 28 29 30 31 32 3
			MASTER VAL

162

The Dimension Statement

The dimensions of an array must be given before it is used in a program.

The Dimension Statement is a non-executable statement which tells the compiler how many elements there are in an array.

Since there are a hundred elements in the array we write:

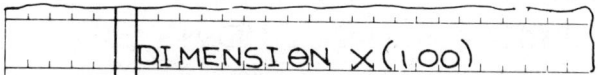

The dimensions of an array can be given in a Type Statement instead of a Dimension Statement and since we shall want to declare the variable MEAN as being Real we can write:

C	STATEMENT NUMBER	CONT.																											
1	2 3 4 5 6		7	8	9	10	11	12	13	14	15	16	17	18	19	20	21	22	23	24	25	26	27	28	29	30
			MASTER VAL																						
			REAL X(100), MEAN																						

Write this on your coding sheet and then assign a value of zero to two locations to hold Σn and $\Sigma(\text{MEAN} - n)^2$.

In Fortran you can read in a whole array using what is known as an implied DO loop

C	STATEMENT NUMBER	CONT.	FORTRAN
			MASTER VAL
			REAL X(100), MEAN
			SUM, SUMSQ = O
41			FORMAT (FO·O)
			READ (40, 41) (X(I), I = 1, 100)

The elements of the array will be read in to successive variables according to the Format shown. That is, the first time the Read Statement is executed I will have a value of 1 and $X(1)$ will be read in. The second time the Read Statement is executed I will have a value 2 and $X(2)$ will be read in and so on until $X(100)$ has been read in.

The statements needed to compute the MEAN are:

```
        DO 33 I = 1, 100
33      SUM = SUM + X(I)
        MEAN = SUM / 100
```

In this DO loop, I takes on every value from 1 to 100 causing $X(1)$, $X(2)$, etc., to be added to the sum.

Write the statements to compute MEAN and then try writing the statements needed to compute the Standard Deviation from

$$\text{STANDARD DEVIATION} = \sqrt{\frac{\Sigma(\text{MEAN} - n)^2}{N}}$$

ANSWER

C	STATEMENT NUMBER	CONT.	FORTRAN
			MASTER VAL
			REAL X(100), MEAN
			SUM, SUMSQ = 0
	41		FORMAT (F0.0)
			READ (40, 41) (X(I), I = 1, 100)
			DO 33 I = 1, 100
	33		SUM = SUM + X(I)
			MEAN = SUM / 100
			DO 34 I = 1, 100
	34		SUMSQ = SUMSQ + (MEAN - X(I)) **2
			STDV = SQRT (SUMSQ / 100)

Output

Now write the Statements to print out the results in the form shown below:

Then write the Statements to finish the program.

ANSWER

C	STATEMENT NUMBER	CONT.	FORTRAN STATEMENT
			MASTER VAL
			REAL X(100), MEAN
			SUM, SUMSQ = 0
	41		FORMAT (F0·0)
			READ (40, 41) (X(I), I = 1, 100)
			DO 33 I = 1, 100
	33		SUM = SUM + X(I)
			MEAN = SUM / 100
			DO 34 I = 1, 100
	34		SUMSQ = SUMSQ + (MEAN - X(I)) **2
			STDV = SQRT (SUMSQ / 100)
	61		FORMAT(7H MEAN =, F6·2 /)
	62		FORMAT(21H STANDARD DEVIATION =, F6·2)
			WRITE (60, 61) MEAN
			WRITE (60, 62) STDV
			STOP
			END

FORM 1/542 (8.64)   © International Computers and Tabulators Limited 1964

1 2 3 4 5	6	7 8 9 10 11 12 13 14 15 16 17 18 19 20 21 22 23 24 25 26 27 28 29 30 31 32 33 34 35 36 37 38 39 40 41
		FINISH

The moment of inertia of a certain angle section about a particular axis is given by the approximate formula

$$A = \frac{4}{3} d^3 t - 2d^2 t^2 + \frac{4}{3} dt^3$$

where d and t are dimensions in inches.

It is required to vary t from ·05 to ·15 in steps of ·01 and to vary d from 1·00 to 4·00 in steps of ·05, calculating A for all possible combinations of t and d. The answers are to be printed as an array having 61 rows corresponding to the values of d and 11 columns corresponding to the values of t.

Here is the start of the program:

C	STATEMENT NUMBER	CONT.	
1 2 3 4 5	6	7 8 9 10 11 12 13 14 15 16 17 18 19 20 21 22 23 24 25 26 27 28 29 30 31 32 33 34	
		PROGRAM (EX11)	
		OUTPUT 60 = LPO	
		END	

1 2 3 4 5	6	7 8 9 10 11 12 13 14 15 16 17 18 19 20 21 22 23 24 25 26 27 28 29 30 31 32 33	
		MASTER CRAN	

We shall require a two-dimensional array of 61 rows and 11 columns to hold the results.

In 1900 Fortran an array can have up to 32 dimensions.

If after the Master Statement we write:

C	STATEMENT NUMBER	CONT.	
1 2 3 4 5	6	7 8 9 10 11 12 13 14 15 16 17 18 19 20 21 22 23 24 25 26 27 28 29 30 31 32 33	
		MASTER CRAN	
		DIMENSION A(61 , 11)	

the compiler will reserve 671 variables to hold the array. The first of the two subscripts gives the number of rows and the second gives the number of columns.

170

Nests of DO's

In Fortran you can have a DO loop within the range of another DO loop. This is called Nesting.

When you have a nest of loops the inner loop MUST be within the range of the outer loop.

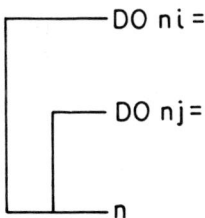

The inner and outer loops may end on the same statement.

The same index must not be used to control two loops when one is nested inside the other, but the index of an outer loop may appear in the indexing parameters of an inner loop.

Provided these rules are observed DO loops can be nested to any depth.

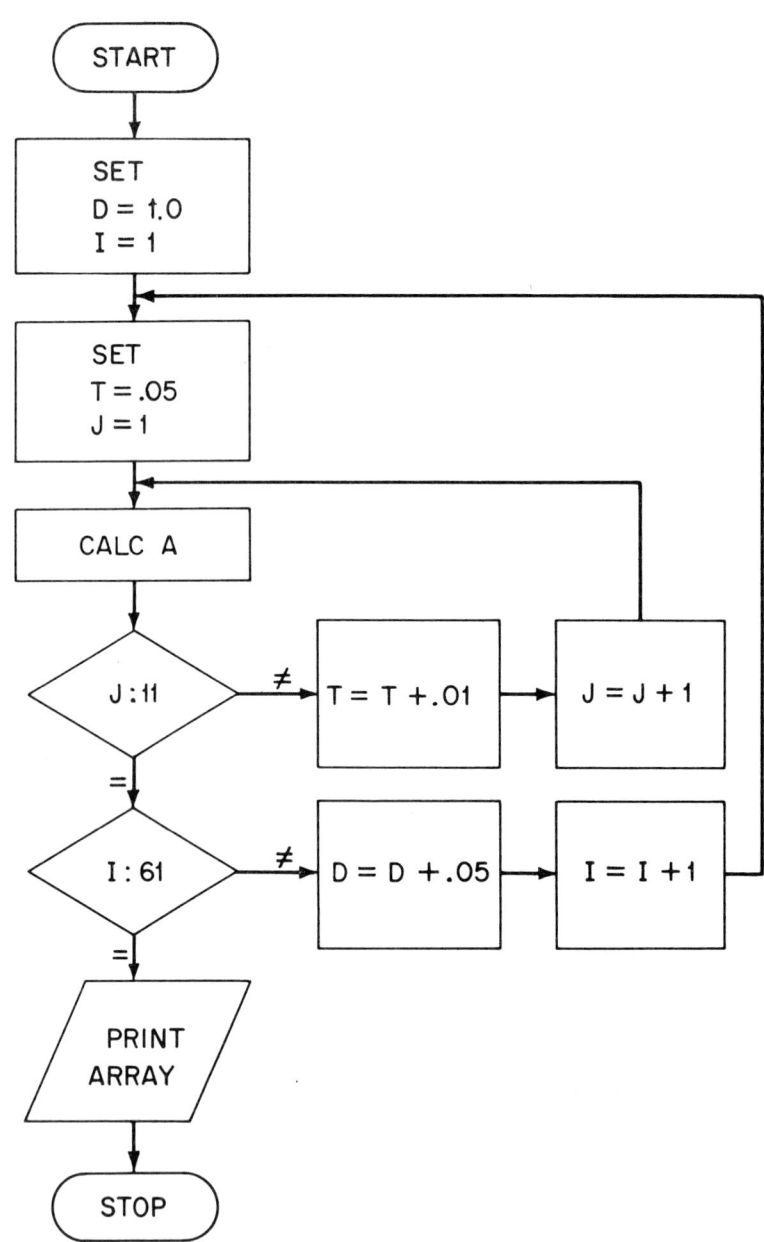

From the flowchart it can be seen that the initial values $D = 1{\cdot}00$ and $I = 1$ are first set up and held unchanged while the inner loop is repeated 11 times with T taking the required values $\cdot05$, $\cdot06$, etc., up to $\cdot15$.

When the inner DO loop is satisfied the elements of the first row of the array, $A(1, 1)$, $A(1, 2)$, $A(1, 3)$, etc., have been calculated and stored.

The outer loop is then traversed to obtain the next value of D and to increment the index I by 1.

The initial values of T and D are then reset and the inner DO loop again repeated 11 times and the second row of the array calculated and stored.

This process is repeated until the outer DO loop has been satisfied.

By referring to the flowchart try writing the arithmetic statements to calculate the array.

FORTRAN STATEMENT

```
      MASTER CRAN
      DIMENSION A(61, 11)
      D = 1.0
      DO 33 I = 1, 61
      T = .05
      DO 34 J = 1, 11
      A(I,J) = 4./3.*D**3*T - 2*D*D*D*T + 4./3.*D*T**3.
   34 T = T + .01
   33 D = D + .05
```

174

You saw in the last example how a complete array could be read in using an implied DO loop. Arrays can be printed out in the same manner.

Our array has 61 rows and 11 columns. Each variable is to be in a field of 10 characters and to have 5 decimal places. So the Format Statement will be:

```
61      FORMAT (11F10.5)
```

To print out the array we simply write:

```
61      FORMAT (11F10.5)
        WRITE (60,61) ((A(I,J),J=1,11), I=1,61)
```

(Note the use of brackets in this Write Statement.)

This will cause the array to be printed out as:

$$A(1, 1), \quad A(1, 2) \quad A(1, 3) \quad \ldots A(1, 11)$$
$$A(2, 1), \quad A(2, 2) \quad A(2, 3) \quad \ldots A(2, 11)$$

$$\cdot \quad \cdot \quad \cdot \quad \cdot \quad \cdot \quad \cdot \quad \cdot \quad \cdot \quad \cdot \quad \cdot \quad \cdot \quad \cdot$$

$$\cdot \quad \cdot \quad \cdot \quad \cdot \quad \cdot \quad \cdot \quad \cdot \quad \cdot \quad \cdot \quad \cdot \quad \cdot$$

$$A(61, 1), A(61, 2), A(61, 3) \ldots A(61, 11)$$

Write the output statements shown and then complete the program.

Here is the complete Master Segment.

176

C	STATEMENT NUMBER	CONT.	FORTRAN STATEMENT
			MASTER CRAN
			DIMENSION A(61, 11)
			D = 1.0
			DO 33 I = 1, 61
			T = .05
			DO 34 J = 1, 11
			A(I,J) = 4./3.*D**3*T − 2*D*D*T*T + 4./3.*D*T**3
	34		T = T + .01
	33		D = D + .05
	61		FORMAT(11F10.5)
			WRITE(60,61) ((A(I,J),J=1,11), I=1,61)
			STOP
			END
			FINISH

The Statement Function

As you have seen, Fortran provides a fairly comprehensive list of Standard Functions, such as SIN, COS and TAN, which you can use simply by writing the correct expression in your program.

You may, however, find in writing a program that some relatively simple calculation keeps recurring throughout the segment of the program.

In Fortran you can define a function within a program segment and then use it whenever it is required within that segment.

EXAMPLE

Let's say that at several points in a program segment you need to use the equation:

$$r = \sqrt{\frac{a}{b + R \sin (2\theta - \alpha)}}$$

A Fortran equivalent of the right-hand side of the equation is:

$$SQRT\ (A\ /\ (B + C* \text{SIN}\ (2*D - E)))$$

To define a Statement Function for this calculation we give the expression a name and list the variable names (called dummy variables) used by it.

If we call this Statement Function **POLAR** the definition will be

$$\text{POLAR}\ (A, B, C, D, E) = SQRT\ (A\ /\ (B + C * \text{SIN}\ (2 * D - E)))$$

This statement causes no calculation to be performed but is simply a non-executable statement to define the function. It must appear before the first executable statement of the segment.

When you want to use the function in the program segment you simply write the name of the function and substitute the variables to be used in place of the dummy variables in the definition.

EXAMPLE

If in the program segment you wanted to find $RMIN$:

where $RMIN = SQRT\,(B\,/\,(C + RMAX * SIN\,(2*T - S)))$

you would write:

$$RMIN = POLAR\,(B, C, RMAX, T, S)$$

substituting the variables in the program for the dummy variables given in the definition.

In choosing a name for a Statement Function you must observe the following rules:

1. The name must not be the same as that of a Standard Function.

2. The name must not be the same as that of any variable appearing in the same segment of the program.

3. The mode of the Statement Function will depend on the first letter of its name unless it is declared by means of a Type Statement; in exactly the same way as a variable.

In selecting the names for the dummy variables used as arguments to define the Statement Function (in the example given, they were $(A, B, C, D$ and $E)$) the following points should be noted:

1. The dummy variables must not be array elements.

2. The dummy variables must be of the same mode as the variables which will replace them when the Statement Function is used in the program.

Apart from this, the names of dummy variables can be anything you choose. It doesn't matter if their names appear as variables in other parts of the segment. No relationship between them is implied.

The actual arguments of the function, which replace the dummy variables when the function is used in the segment, may be variables or array elements, indeed—they may be any expression as long as each one has the same mode as its dummy argument.

EXAMPLE

The dummy variables we used to define the Statement Function were

$$A, B, C, D, E$$

and the actual variables used in the program were

$$B, C, RMAX, T, S$$

The dummy variables B and C used in the definition have no connection with the variables B and C which replaced the dummy variables A and B.

QUESTION

1. (a) If the co-ordinates of two points in space are x_1, y_1, z_1 and x_2, y_2, z_2 then the distance between the points is given by:

$$D = \sqrt{(x_1 - x_2)^2 + (y_1 - y_2)^2 + (z_1 - z_2)^2}$$

Write a Statement Function for this computation.

(b) Use the Statement Function you have defined to calculate the distance between two points A and B whose co-ordinates are represented by the arrays $A(I)$, $B(I)$ respectively, the maximum value of I being 3.

Store the answer in the location SPACE.

ANSWER

1. (*a*) DIST $(X1, Y1, Z1, X2, Y2, Z2)$
   $= SQRT((X1 - X2)**2 + (Y1 - Y2)**2 + (Z1 - Z2)**2)$

1. (*b*) SPACE = DIST $(A(1), A(2), A(3), B(1), B(2), B(3))$

Function Segments

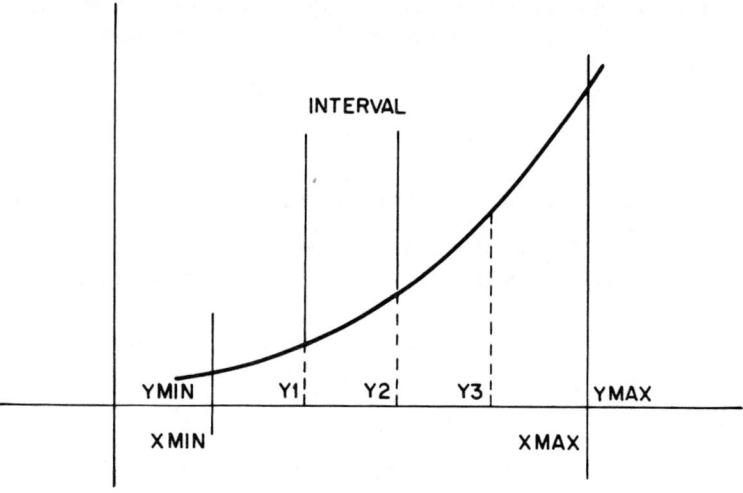

If $y = ax^r + bx + c$ and we wanted to find

$$\int_{xmin}^{xmax} y \, dx$$

a good approximation of the definite integral could be found using Simpson's Rule.

To apply Simpson's Rule to find the area under a curve, we divide the curve up into an even number of strips and the area is given by the formula:

AREA $= \frac{1}{3} \times$ interval $\times$ (the sum of the first and last ordinates

+ 4 times the sum of the odd ordinates
+ 2 times the sum of the remaining even ordinates)

i.e. if the area were divided up into 4 strips:

$$\text{AREA} = \frac{1}{3} \times \text{INTERVAL}$$
$$\times (YMIN + YMAX + 4(Y1 + Y3) + 2(Y2))$$

The more strips the area is divided into the more accurate our answer will be.

Since a computer can perform calculations at very high speeds it will cause no hardship if we divide the area into, say, 1000 or even 10000 strips.

But since normal accuracy of the computer is to 11 significant figures it would be pointless to use too many divisions.

Write a section of a program to calculate the area under the curve

$$y = ax^r + bx + c$$

Assume that the values of A, B, C and R and the limits of X have already been read in.

Omit the output and terminal statements.

You will find it useful to set up a Statement Function for

$$y = ax^r + bx + c$$

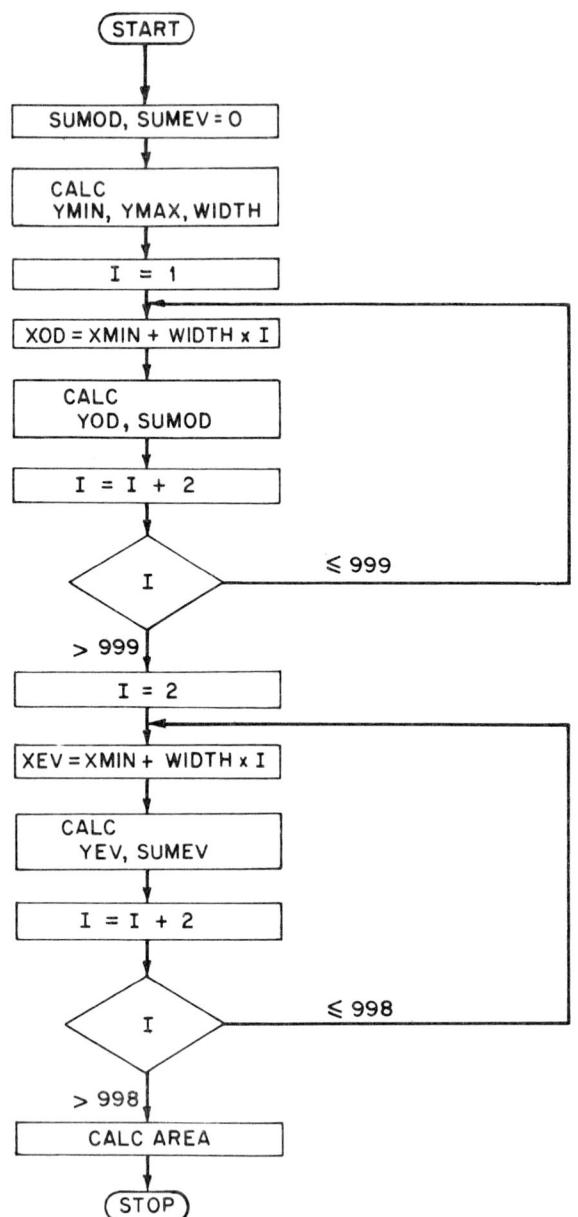

```
EQ(A,B,C,R,X) = A*X**R + B*X + C
SUMOD, SUMEV = 0
YMIN = EQ(A,B,C,R,XMIN)
YMAX = EQ(A,B,C,R,XMAX)
WIDTH = (XMAX - XMIN)/1000
DO 33 I = 1, 999, 2
XOD = XMIN + WIDTH * I
YOD = EQ(A,B,C,R,XOD)
SUMOD = SUMOD + YOD
DO 34 I = 2, 998, 2
XEV = XMIN + WIDTH * I
YEV = EQ(A,B,C,R,XEV)
SUMEV = SUMEV + YEV
AREA = WIDTH/3.0 *(YMIN + YMAX + A*SUMOD + 2*SUMEV)
```

Statement numbers: 33 (SUMOD = SUMOD + YOD), 34 (SUMEV = SUMEV + YEV)

The Function Segment

Although the Statement Function is useful, it does have two important limitations:

1. The Statement Function may only be used in the segment in which it is defined.

2. It is limited to one statement.

When writing a program you may find that you need to do a certain computation at several points in the program.

You can set up a special function to perform these calculations by writing a Function Segment, which is used in the same way as a Standard Function.

EXAMPLE

At several points of a program we want to find the definite integral of $y = ax^r + bx + c$.

So, let's change the routine we have just written to compute

$$\int_{x\text{min}}^{x\text{max}} y \, dx$$

into a Function Segment.

If we had written a complete program we would have supplied values for A, B, C, R, XMIN and XMAX and would have output the final value of the variable AREA.

In a Function Segment A, B, C, R, XMIN and XMAX are the arguments of the Function and AREA is the name of the Function Segment. So to define the routine as being a Function Segment we write:

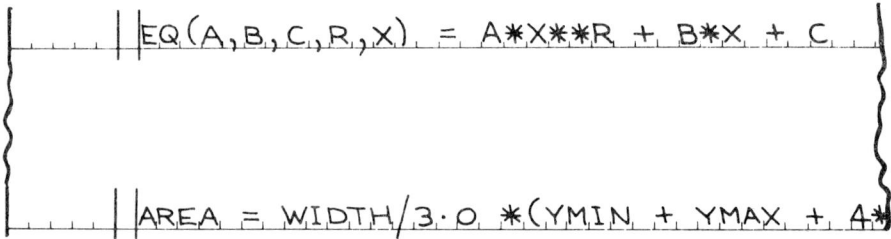

We follow this with the routine to compute AREA:

After which we write the Return Statement which transfers control back to the calling segment:

and as with all segments in Fortran we must have an END Statement:

192

When the Function Segment is used in the program it is simply written in with the correct variables in the same way as a Statement Function.

EXAMPLE

To calculate the area under the curve $XW^s + YW + Z$ between the limits A and B, multiply the result by 2π and store the result in ANS.

We write

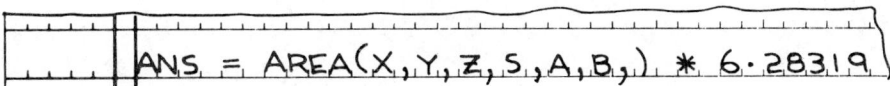

Before using Function Segments we must look more closely at the rules governing Function Names, etc.

193

Function Segment Names

The name you choose for a Function Segment must not be the same as that of a Standard Function or of any other segment in the program.

As you have seen, the name of the Function Segment, in this case AREA, must be the same as that of the variable whose final value we want as the value of the function. This name must not appear in a non-executable statement in the Function Segment. The name must, of course, appear at least once on the left-hand side of the routine.

The mode of a Function Segment is given by the initial letter of its name or the mode can be given in the definition of the Function Segment.

For example, if we had called the Function Segment we wrote, INTEGRAL, we would have written:

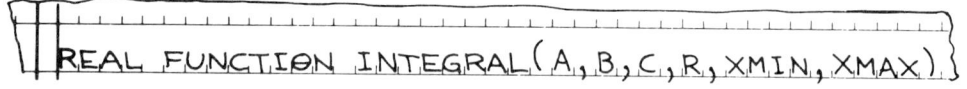

The mode of the Function would then have to be given in a Type Statement in any segment in which it was used.

194

Function Segment Arguments

The arguments of a Function Segment, in this case A, B, C, R, XMIN and XMAX, are dummy variables and are used only to define the Function Segment. They have no relationship to any other variables of the same name in any other segment.

The dummy variables must be of the same mode as the variables which will replace them when the Function Segment is being used.

The mode of a dummy variable is given by the first letter of its name, or it can be declared in a Type Statement in the Function Segment.

The Return Statement

A Function Segment must have at least one Return Statement.

The Return Statement causes control to be transferred back to the point in the segment which called the function.

When the Return Statement is executed the value of the variable with the same name as the Function, in this case AREA, will be the value of the Function Segment.

There can be more than one Return Statement in a Function Segment and the Return Statement need not be at the end of the routine. This is useful when the routine involves conditional branches.

QUESTION

Write a complete program to find the largest of 9 variables, O, P, Q, R, S, T, U, V, W, incorporating a Function Segment which finds the largest of 3 variables.

The input data is on cards with 3 variables per card and can be input using Free Format.

The result is to be output thus:

THE LARGEST VALUE IS $XXX.XX$

Remember that the Finish Statement comes after the last segment of the program.

ANSWER

C	STATEMENT NUMBER	CONT.	
	1 2 3 4 5	6	7 8 9 10 11 12 13 14 15 16 17 18 19 20 21 22 23 24 25 26 27 28 29 30 31 32 33 34 3
			PROGRAM (EX12)
			INPUT 50 = CRO
			OUTPUT 60 = LPO
			END

C	STATEMENT NUMBER	CONT.	FORTRAN STA
	1 2 3 4 5	6	7 8 9 10 11 12 13 14 15 16 17 18 19 20 21 22 23 24 25 26 27 28 29 30 31 32 33 34 35 36 37 38 39 40 41
			MASTER FIND
			REAL MAX
	51		FORMAT (3F0.0)
			READ (50 , 51) O,P,Q,R,S,T,U,V,W
			X = MAX(O, P, Q)
			Y = MAX(R, S, T)
			Z = MAX(U, V, W)
			BIG = MAX(X, Y, Z)
			WRITE (60 , 61) BIG
	61		FORMAT(22H THE LARGEST VALUE IS ,F7.2)
			STOP
			END

198

C	STATEMENT NUMBER	CONT.		FOR
1 2 3 4 5		6	7 8 9 10 11 12 13 14 15 16 17 18 19 20 21 22 23 24 25 26 27 28 29 30 31 32 33 34 35 36	
			REAL FUNCTION MAX (A, B, C)	
			MAX = A	
			IF (MAX - B) 2, 0, 0	
4			IF (MAX - C) 3, 0, 0	
			RETURN	
2			MAX = B	
			GO TO 4	
3			MAX = C	
			RETURN	
			END	
			FINISH	

The Program Description Segment

In 1900 Fortran we need a Program Description Segment to assign labels to the Peripherals. But since it varies little from program to program we shall omit from now on and adopt the following convention:

Label 40—the Paper Tape Reader.

Label 50—the Card reader.

Label 60—the Line Printer.

Data Types

So far all our work has been done with data of either Real or Integer mode.

1900 Fortran can in fact handle six types of data, these are:

> INTEGER
>
> REAL
>
> DOUBLE PRECISION
>
> COMPLEX
>
> LOGICAL
>
> TEXT

Type Statements

As you know, the mode of Integer and Real variables can be declared either by the initial letter of the variable name or by a Type Statement.

The mode of Double Precision, Complex and Logical variables must be declared by a Type Statement.

C	STATEMENT NUMBER	CONT.		FORT
			DOUBLE PRECISION PI, EXP	
			COMPLEX FORE, ELECTRO	
			LOGICAL QI, INT	

There are no Text variables as such, since variables of any mode can be used to hold data in character form.

The various types of values in Fortran are held in Storage Locations in the Computer's Central Processor.

Integer, Real and Logical values occupy one Storage Location.

Complex and Double Precision values occupy two Storage Locations.

$$\left[\begin{array}{l} \text{Note: The basic unit of core-store in the I.C.T. 1900} \\ \text{series computers is the 1900 Word.} \\ \text{One Fortran Storage Location equals two 1900 Words.} \end{array}\right]$$

Double Precision Numbers

Like a Real number, a Double Precision Number lies in the approximate range

$$-5\cdot6 \times 10^{76} \text{ to } 5\cdot6 \times 10^{76}$$

and is held in floating point form.

It is held to an accuracy of 20 significant figures (a Real number is held to 11).

Double Precision Constants

A constant is regarded as being of Double Precision mode if it is a number written with or without a decimal point and followed by an exponent, introduced by the letter D with a one or two digit, positive or negative power of ten.

For example:

$$53D +2 \text{ meaning } \quad 53 \times 10^2$$
$$\cdot23D -3 \text{ meaning } \quad \cdot23 \times 10^{-3}$$
$$-4\cdot1D -5 \text{ meaning } -4\cdot1 \times 10^{-5}$$

are all Double Precision Constants.

As you see they are very similar to one of the forms of Real Numbers.

QUESTION

Write the following numbers as Double Precision Constants:

1. 12345678901234567890
2. ·31415927E + 1
3. 6
4. —·031

ANSWER

1. $\cdot 1234567890123456789D + 20$

2. $\cdot 31415927D + 1$

3. $\cdot 6D + 1$

4. $-\cdot 31D - 1$

Your answers may differ slightly from the ones shown but they must have been written with an exponent introduced by the letter D.

EXAMPLE

The magnitudes of two vectors A and B are punched on a card as shown.

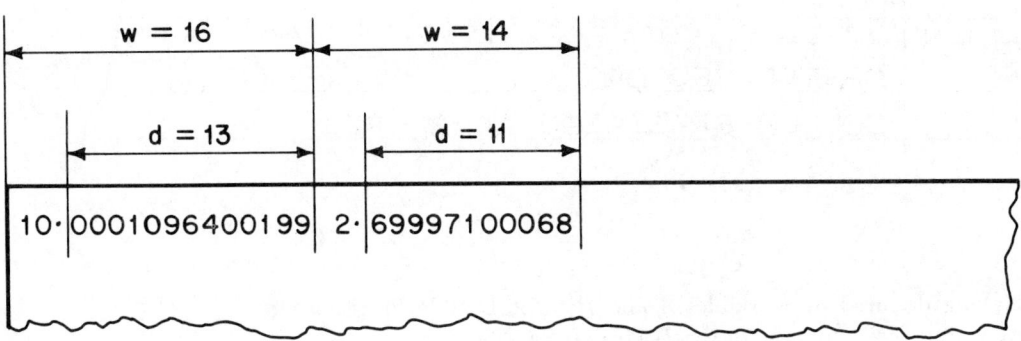

We have to write a program which will compute the resultant of these vectors.

$$RES = \sqrt{A^2 + B^2}$$

and print out the answer to 12 significant figures.

Before turning over, write the Master Statement and make any necessary Type Statements. Remember any variable which is to hold a Double Precision value must be declared to be Double Precision.

The D Format Specification

C	STATEMENT NUMBER	CONT.	FORTRAN STA
1 2 3 4 5	6	7 8 9 10 11 12 13 14 15 16 17 18 19 20 21 22 23 24 25 26 27 28 29 30 31 32 33 34 35 36 37 38 39 40 4

```
          MASTER VECTOR
          DOUBLE PRECISION A, B, RES
```

Having declared the variables *A* and *B* to be Double Precision we can input their values with the *D* Format Specification.

On input, the *D* Format caused values in form to be converted to Double Precision form.

So, the Format Statement will be:

```
51    FORMAT (D16.13, D14.11)
      READ (50, 51) A, B
```

As you can see from Appendix A, there is a comprehensive list of Double Precision Standard Functions.

C	STATEMENT NUMBER	CONT.	
			MASTER VECTOR
			DOUBLE PRECISION A, B, RES
	51		FORMAT (D16.13, D14.11)
			READ(50, 51) A, B
			RES = DSQRT(A*A + B*B)

After calculating the resultant we output its value using the D Format. On output the effect of the D Format is very similar to that of the E Format. That is, it prints the number as a decimal fraction less than 1·0 but greater than or equal to 0·1 and with an exponent.

We want to output the value of RES with 12 significant figures.

Say the value of RES was 10·6660000968 then the Format

$$D20·12$$

will cause it to be printed out thus:

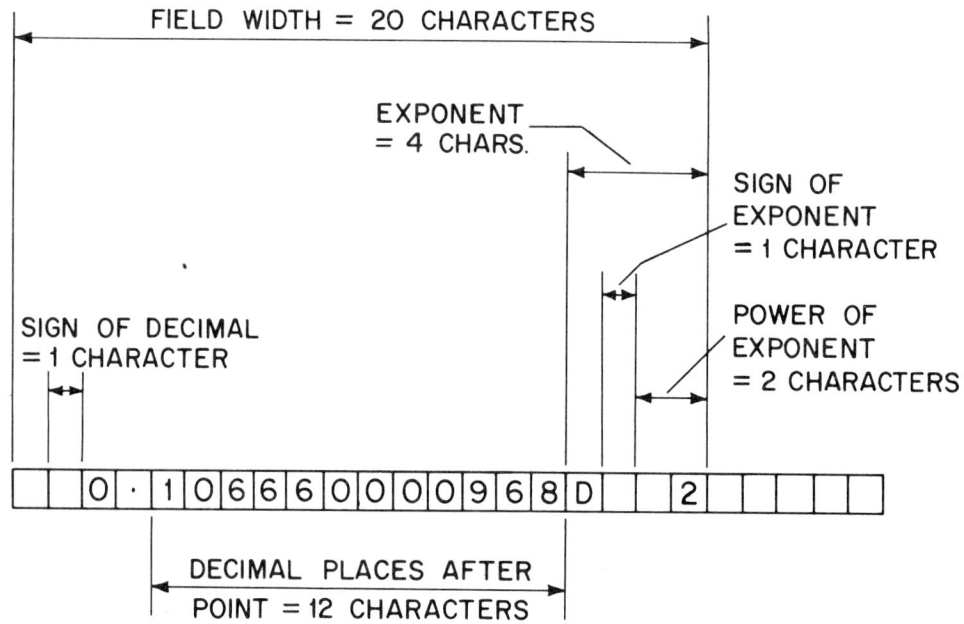

The following points will be noted from the diagram.

If the sign of either the decimal fraction or the exponent is positive its character position is left blank.

If the power of the exponent is less than ten the first character position of the power is left blank.

As with the *E*, *F* and *I* Formats the number is printed as far to the right as possible.

We can now complete the coding of our program by writing:

C	STATEMENT NUMBER	CONT.		FC
			MASTER VECTOR	
			DOUBLE PRECISION A, B, RES	
	51		FORMAT(D16.13, D14.11)	
			READ(50, 51) A, B	
			RES = DSQRT(A*A + B*B)	
	61		FORMAT(D20.12)	
			WRITE(60, 61) RES	
			STOP	
			END	
			FINISH	

Mixed Mode Arithmetic

Double Precision variables can be mixed in an expression with Real and Integer variables, but not with Complex. The final value of the expression will be Double Precision but some of the individual terms may not be evaluated in Double Precision mode.

For example:

If A and B are Real variables and X and Y are Double Precision then, in the expression:

$$A/B + X/Y$$

A/B will be evaluated in Real mode and then converted to Double Precision before the expression is evaluated.

QUESTION

We can compute e from the series

$$e = 1 + \frac{1}{1!} + \frac{1}{2!} + \frac{1}{3!} + \cdots$$

Write a program which will compute e to 20 decimal places and print out the answer.

ANSWER

C	STATEMENT NUMBER	CONT.	FORTRAN
1 2 3 4 5		6	7 8 9 10 11 12 13 14 15 16 17 18 19 20 21 22 23 24 25 26 27 28 29 30 31 32 33 34 35 36 37 38 3
			MASTER EXPO
			DOUBLE PRECISION E, N, TERM
			E = 2D+0
			N = 2D+0
			TERM = 1D+0
21			TERM = TERM / N
			E = E + TERM
			IF (TERM - 1D-20) 22, 0, 0
			N = N + 1
			GO TO 21
61			FORMAT (D28.20)
22			WRITE (60, 61) E
			STOP
			END
			FINISH

Complex Numbers

Mathematically a complex number is considered to have the form:

$$a + ib$$

In Fortran, the two parts of a Complex number are held in two Storage Locations as two Real numbers. Consequently, both parts of a Complex number can be any number in the range

$$-5{\cdot}6 \times 10^{76} \text{ to } 5{\cdot}6 \times 10^{76}$$

Complex Constants

A Complex constant is written as two Real constants, separated by a comma and enclosed in brackets.

For example:

$$(6\cdot5, \ 2\cdot3) \text{ meaning } 6\cdot5 + 2\cdot3i$$
$$(3E - 2, \ 6E1) \text{ meaning } \cdot03 + 60i$$
$$(\cdot3E - 1, \ -6\cdot2) \text{ meaning } \cdot03 - 6\cdot2i$$
$$(-4\cdot \ , \ -1\cdot \ ) \text{ meaning } -4 - i$$

are all Complex constants.

The two parts of the constant can be any of the forms of Real numbers, but they must be Real numbers.

So, a whole number must be written as a Real number.

For example:

$$3 + 2i \text{ must be written as}$$
$$(3\cdot \ , \ 2\cdot \ )$$
$$\text{or } (3\cdot0, \ 2\cdot0)$$
$$\text{or even } (\cdot3E1, \ \cdot2E1)$$

QUESTION

Write the following complex numbers in Fortran notation:

1. $1 + i$
2. $\cdot 00005 - \cdot 0016i$
3. $-63 \cdot 5 + 4i$
4. $3 + 2i$

ANSWER

1. $(1 \cdot 0, 1 \cdot 0)$
2. $(\cdot 5E - 4, -\cdot 16E - 2)$
3. $(-63 \cdot 5, 4 \cdot 0)$
4. $(3 \cdot 0, 2 \cdot 0)$

If your answers differ from the ones shown, judge for yourself if they comply with the rules.

EXAMPLE

The two components of Impedance in a circuit are represented by the two parts of a complex number. The total impedance of circuits in parallel is given by the sum of reciprocals of the individual impedances:

$$Z = \frac{1}{z_1} + \frac{1}{z_2} + \frac{1}{z_3} \ldots$$

We have to write a program which will find the total impedance of ten circuits in parallel.

Two individual pairs of values are punched on a card thus:

Start the program by writing the Master Statement and making any necessary Type Statements. Then set to zero the variable to hold the sum.

ANSWER

C	STATEMENT NUMBER	CONT.																																FC
1	2 3 4 5	6	7 8 9 10 11 12 13 14 15 16 17 18 19 20 21 22 23 24 25 26 27 28 29 30 31 32 33 34 35																																

```
      MASTER IMP
      COMPLEX Z(10), SUM
      SUM = (0.0, 0.0)
```

Input of Complex Variables

Since a Complex variable consists of two Real numbers it needs two E or F Format Specifications for Input or Output.

Taking each field separately the Format of one record is:

$$F5\cdot2, F6\cdot3, F5\cdot2, F6\cdot3$$

and we could read in the two complex variables on the card by writing:

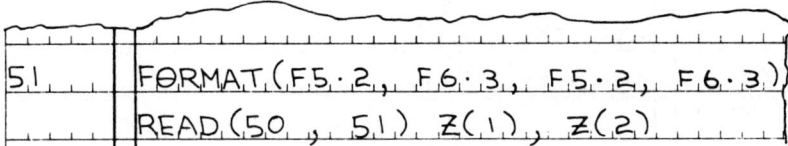

```
51    FORMAT (F5·2, F6·3, F5·2, F6·3)
      READ (50, 51) Z(1), Z(2)
```

Since each variable has the same format we can write

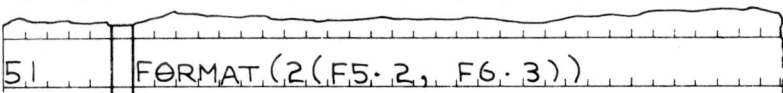

```
51    FORMAT (2(F5·2, F6·3))
```

and read in the complete array by an implied DO loop.

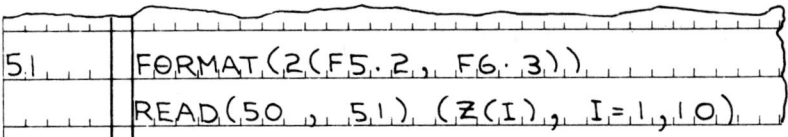

```
51    FORMAT (2(F5·2, F6·3))
      READ (50, 51) (Z(I), I=1,10)
```

Now write the arithmetic statements to compute the sum of the reciprocals of the Impedance.

ANSWER

C	STATEMENT NUMBER	CONT.																													FC
1 2 3 4 5	6	7 8 9 10 11 12 13 14 15 16 17 18 19 20 21 22 23 24 25 26 27 28 29 30 31 32 33 34 35																														

```
       MASTER IMP
       COMPLEX Z(10), SUM
       SUM = (0.0, 0.0)
51     FORMAT(2(F5.2, F6.3))
       READ(50, 51)(Z(I), I=1,10)
       DO 33 I = 1, 10
33     SUM = SUM + 1.0/Z(I)
```

222

To print out the sum in the form

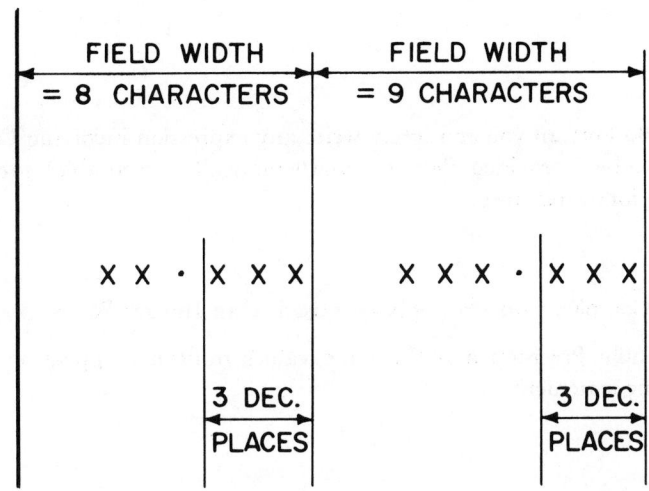

We would write

```
61       FORMAT (F8·3 , F9·3)
         WRITE (60 , 61) SUM
```

and then complete the program

```
         STOP
         END
         FINISH
```

Operations on Complex Numbers

In 1900 Fortran you can freely write any expression involving Complex values (provided they are mathematically acceptable) subject to the following rules:

1. A Complex value can only be raised to an Integer Power.

2. Double Precision and Complex values must not appear in the same statement.

A list of the Complex Standard Functions is given in Appendix A.

QUESTION

Write a program which will compute:

$$(a + ib)^{3/2}$$

and print out the result in the form:

$$
\begin{array}{ll}
XXX.XX & XXX.XX \\
XXX.XX & XXX.XX \\
XXX.XX & XXX.XX
\end{array}
$$

The input data is on cards in the form:

$$XXX.XX \quad XXX.XX$$

The end of data is marked by a card on which the real part of the number is 999·99.

ANSWER

C	STATEMENT NUMBER	CONT.	FORTRAN STATEM
			MASTER PLEX
			COMPLEX ZEB ROZEB
51			FORMAT (2F8.2)
89			READ (50, 51) ZEB
			IF (REAL (ZEB) — 999.99) 0, 99, 0
			ROZEB = ZEB **3
			ROZEB = CSQRT (ROZEB)
			WRITE (60, 61) ROZEB
61			FORMAT (2F8.2)
			GO TO 89
99			STOP
			END
			FINISH

Text Data

In many programs part of the input data will be information in character form which requires no processing but which is to appear on the output document.

As we have said, variables of any sort can be used to hold data in character form.

One Storage Location can hold up to eight characters.

So, Integer, Real and Logical variables can hold up to eight characters and Double Precision and Complex, sixteen.

EXAMPLE

The first three items on a punched card are the date, an engine type and a part number.

DATE	TYPE	PARTNO	
8 CHAR.	6 CHAR.	7 CHAR.	
12/09/66	DRONGO	BX 6014	

This information is to be printed out as part of the output document.

For this example we shall ignore the other fields.

The A Format

Data in character form is input and output by the _A_ Format.

The first item on the card is the date which is in a field of 8 characters.

To read this into the variable DATE, we write:

```
51      FORMAT (A8,
        READ (50, 51) DATE,
```

The characters will be held in the variable like this:

DATE

```
1 2 / 0 9 / 6 6
```

The next item is in a field of six characters, so we write:

```
51      FORMAT(A8, A6,
        READ(50, 51) DATE, TYPE,
```

It will be held in the variable TYPE like this:

TYPE

| D | R | O | N | G | O | | |

That is, the characters are read into the six leftmost character positions of the variable. The remaining two positions are filled with blanks.

And to complete the statements we read the last item into the variable PARTNO.

```
51      FORMAT(A8, A6, A7)
        READ(50, 51) DATE, TYPE, PARTNO
```

PARTNO

| B | X | | 6 | 0 | 1 | 4 | |

Again the remaining character position is filled with a blank.

230

Output

We want to output the characters in the form:

12/09/66   DRONGO   BX 6014

There are a variety of ways we can achieve this output, but perhaps the simplest is to reproduce the input format, adding in space characters where required:

```
61    FORMAT(1X, A8, 2X, A6, 2X, A7)
      WRITE(60, 61)DATE, TYPE, PARTNO
```

QUESTION

1. Write the statements needed to input the following text data from a card

REGNO	TYPE	WT	
2AX 234	GAZELLE	325·5	
w = 7	w = 8	w = 6	

and show how the data will be held in the variables.

2. Write the statements needed to output the data in the form:

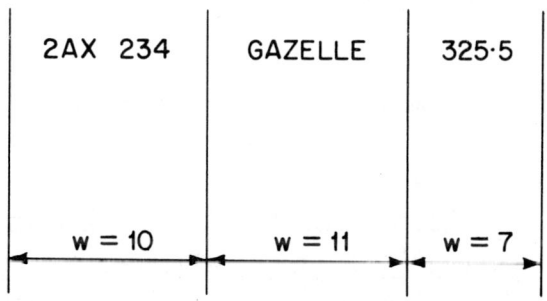

233

ANSWER

1.

```
5,1      FORMAT (A7, A8, A6)
         READ (50, 51) REGNØ, TYPE, WT
```

```
           REGNO
         2 A X   2 3 4
```

```
            TYPE
         G A Z E L L E
```

```
             WT
           3 2 5   5
```

2.

```
6,1      FORMAT (3X,A7,3X,A8,1X,A6)
         WRITE (60, 61) REGNØ, TYPE,
```

or if you used the spaces in the variables you could write:

```
6,1      FORMAT (3X,A8,2X,A8,1X,A8)
         WRITE (60, 61) REGNØ, TYPE, WT
```

Text Data in Arrays

There will often be more characters in an item of data than can be held in a single variable.

Just as a variable of any mode can be used to hold text data, so can an array. If we define an array with sufficient elements to hold the characters, we can read the whole item .into that array with an Implied DO Loop.

EXAMPLE

Let's say that the first 24 positions on a card give a person's name.

MARILYN LOUISE HOWARD

An array with three elements will be big enough to hold the data.

```
       DIMENSION NAME(3)
```

We can now write:

```
51     FORMAT (3A8)
       READ (50, 51) (NAME(I), I=1, 3)
```

The first 8 characters will be read into NAME (1) and the remaining characters will be read into succeeding elements of the array.

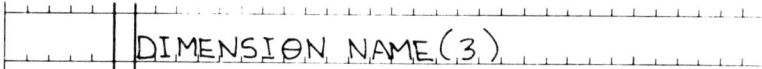

Unused character positions in the last variable are filled with blanks.

The same Format is used for output.

QUESTION

The first 24 character positions on a card give the name of a town and the next 16 positions give the county:

PRINCES RISBOROUGH   BUCKINGHAMSHIRE

Write the statements needed to input this information and show how the data will be held in the arrays.

ANSWER

```
       DIMENSION T(3), C(2)
51     FORMAT (3A8, 2A8)
       READ(50, 51)(T(I), I=1,3),C(1),C(2)
```

P	R	I	N	C	E	S		R	I	S	B	O	R	O	U	G	H						

B	U	C	K	I	N	G	H	A	M	S	H	I	R	E	

Logical Values

If we declare a variable to be of the mode Logical we can fill it with a string of 1 bits or of 0 bits.

By convention a string of 1 bits is said to represent the value of ·TRUE· and a string of 0 bits to represent the value ·FALSE·.

Logical Constants

The two Logical constants are

·TRUE·

and

·FALSE·

Note the full stops. They are an essential part of the constants.

EXAMPLE

We would use the constants to give initial value to Logical variables:

```
LOGICAL QUER, INT
QUER = ·TRUE·
INT = ·FALSE·
```

EXAMPLE

The personal details of each employee of a firm are on a punched card. The 37th column of the card is punched to represent the sex of the employee.

It has been punched with a T to represent male and with an F to represent female.

We have been asked to write a program to find what percentage of the employees are men.

As you shall see when we read a card we have used the Logical value ·TRUE· to represent male and ·FALSE· to represent female. So if we read the sex of the employee into SEX we must declare it to be a Logical variable.

C	STATEMENT NUMBER	CONT.		FC
			MASTER EMP	
			REAL MEN	
			LOGICAL SEX	
			MEN, TOTAL = 0	

The L Format Specification

As you might suspect the *L* Format Specification is used to input and output Logical variables.

On the input document we can represent the values ·TRUE· and ·FALSE· in a variety of ways but essentially the letter 'T' represents ·TRUE· and the letter 'F' represents ·FALSE·.

We want to skip the first 36 character positions on the card and read in the Logical value in a field of 1 character position at the 37th.

C	STATEMENT NUMBER	CONT.		FC
			MASTER EMP	
			REAL MEN	
			LOGICAL SEX	
			MEN, TOTAL = 0	
	51		FORMAT (36X, L1)	
			READ (50, 51) SEX	

Logical IF Statement

We now want to test the value of SEX to see if it is ·TRUE· or ·FALSE·.

Just as we can test if an Arithmetic expression is negative, zero or positive with an Arithmetic IF Statement, we can test if a Logical expression is ·TRUE· or ·FALSE· with a Logical IF Statement.

If SEX is ·TRUE· we want to add one to the value of MEN.

```
IF (SEX) MEN = MEN + 1
```

If sex is FALSE we want to leave the value of MEN unchanged and go on to the next statement which adds one to the TOTAL.

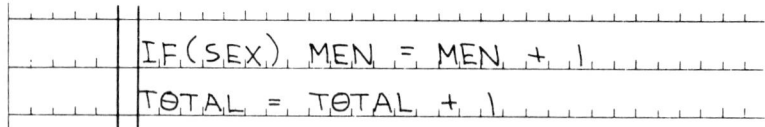

```
IF (SEX) MEN = MEN + 1
TOTAL = TOTAL + 1
```

If we assume that we know that the total number of employees is 1837 we can now complete the coding of the program.

C	STATEMENT NUMBER	CONT.		FC
			MASTER EMP	
			REAL MEN	
			LOGICAL SEX	
			MEN, TOTAL = 0	
51			FORMAT (36X, L1)	
89			READ (50, 51) SEX	
			IF (SEX) MEN = MEN + 1	
			TOTAL = TOTAL + 1	
			IF (TOTAL - 1837) 89, 0, 0	
			PERM = MEN * 100 /TOTAL	
61			FORMAT (8H %MEN =,F5.1)	
			WRITE (60, 61) PERM	
			STOP	
			END	
			FINISH	

The L Format

Let's say we have to input the values of two Logical variables A and B. The values are punched on a card as shown.

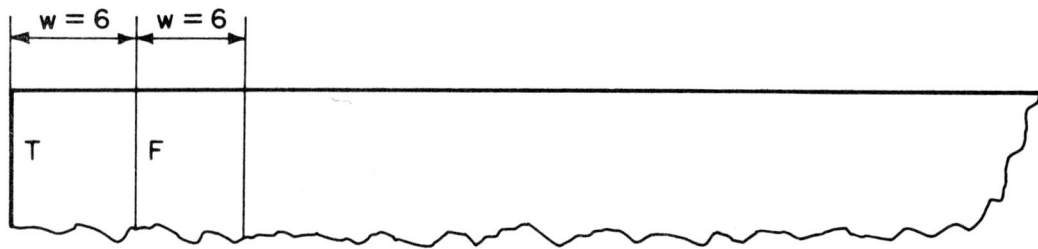

To input the values we write

```
          LOGICAL A, B
5 1       FORMAT (2L6)
          READ (50, 51) A, B
```

The first non-blank character in the field must be the value of the variable, either T or F. Any characters after the T or F are ignored. So, we could have punched on the card, say

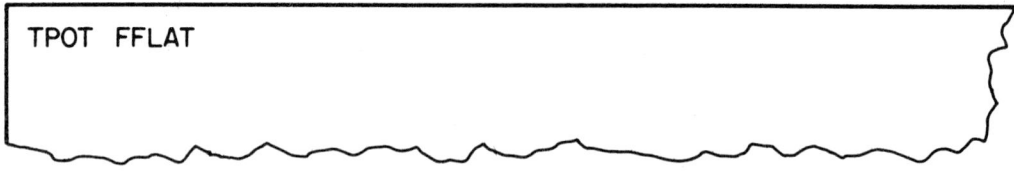

without affecting the values.

To output the values of the two Logical variables we could write

```
6 1      FORMAT (2L4)
         WRITE (60, 61), A, B
```

Each variable would be output in a field of 4 character positions.

Since A has a value of $\cdot$TRUE$\cdot$ it will be output as 3 blank positions followed by the letter T:

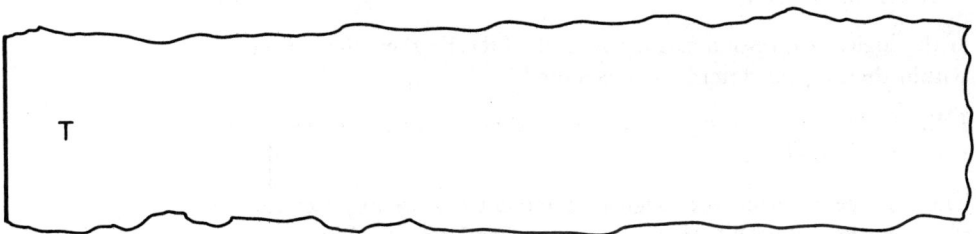

B has a value of $\cdot$FALSE$\cdot$. It will be output as 3 blanks followed by the letter F:

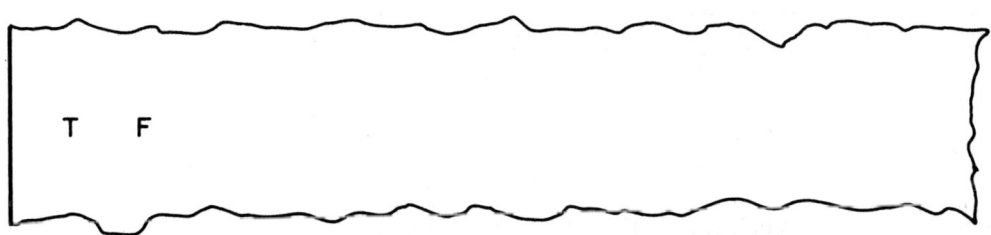

The Logical IF Statement

The Logical IF Statement has the general form

IF (logical expression) statement
next statement

The logical expression can be any expression which has a value of $\cdot$TRUE$\cdot$ or $\cdot$FALSE$\cdot$.

If the logical expression has a value of $\cdot$TRUE$\cdot$ then the statement within the Logical statement is executed.

If the Logical expression has a value of $\cdot$FALSE$\cdot$ then the next statement is executed.

The statement within the Logical statement can be any executable statement except a DO statement or another Logical IF Statement.

QUESTION

The first four characters on a card give a logical value.

Write a program which will read in this value and test whether it's ·TRUE· or ·FALSE·. If it is ·TRUE· print out TRUE and FALSE if it is ·FALSE·.

ANSWER

C	STATEMENT NUMBER	CONT.	FC
1 2 3 4 5	6	7 8 9 10 11 12 13 14 15 16 17 18 19 20 21 22 23 24 25 26 27 28 29 30 31 32 33 34 35	

```
              MASTER IMP
              LOGICAL QUI
51            FORMAT(L4)
              READ(50, 51) QUI
              IF(QUI) GO TO 88
              WRITE(60, 62) QUI
              GO TO 99
88            WRITE(60, 61) QUI
99            STOP
61            FORMAT(10X,L1,3HRUE)
62            FORMAT(10X,L1,4HALSE)
              END
              FINISH
```

Logical Expressions

Logical Elements can be combined by the Logical Operators.

The Logical Operators are:

·NOT·
·AND·
·OR·

Note: The full stops are essential.

Like Logical variables, Logical expressions can have only the values
of ·TRUE· or ·FALSE·.

EXAMPLE

If *A* and *B* are Logical variables then the Logical expression:

·NOT· A

will have a value of ·TRUE· if *A* is ·FALSE·.
It will have a value of ·FALSE· if *A* is ·TRUE·.

The Logical expression

A ·AND· B

will have a value of ·TRUE· if both *A* and *B* are ·TRUE·. It will have a value of ·FALSE· if:

1. Either *A* or *B* is ·FALSE·.
2. Both *A* and *B* are ·FALSE·.

The Logical expression

A ·OR· B

will have a value of ·TRUE· if:

1. Either *A* or *B* is ·TRUE·.
2. Both *A* and *B* are ·TRUE·.

It will have a value of FALSE if both *A* and *B* are ·FALSE·.

QUESTION

If A and B both have a value of ·TRUE· and X and Y both have a value of ·FALSE·, what is the value of the following expressions?

1. ·NOT· X

2. A ·OR· X

3. X ·AND· B

4. Y ·OR· X

5. A ·AND· B

ANSWER

1. ·TRUE·
2. ·TRUE·
3. ·FALSE·
4. ·FALSE·
5. ·TRUE·

Complex Logical Expressions

Logical expressions may contain more than one Logical Operator.

The Logical **·AND·**

and the Logical **·OR·**

must be preceded by a Logical element and followed by a Logical element, or by the Logical **·NOT·**.

EXAMPLE

$$A \cdot \text{AND} \cdot B \cdot \text{OR} \cdot C$$
$$A \cdot \text{OR} \cdot B \cdot \text{AND} \cdot \cdot \text{NOT} \cdot X$$

Conversely, the Logical **·NOT·** must not be preceded by an element but can be preceded by a Logical **·AND·** or **·OR·**. It must be followed by a Logical element.

EXAMPLE

$$\cdot \text{NOT} \cdot A \cdot \text{OR} \cdot B$$
$$B \cdot \text{AND} \cdot \cdot \text{NOT} \cdot A$$

Order of Evaluation

As with the Arithmetic operators, the Logical operators have an order of evaluation.

When the computer is evaluating an expression it first evaluates all the expressions enclosed in brackets and evaluates the complete expression in the sequence:

·NOT·

·AND·

·OR·

That is **·NOT·** operations are performed first, followed by **·AND·**, followed by **·OR·**.

Within each of these classes the order is from left to right.

QUESTION

If A, B and C have a value of $\cdot$TRUE$\cdot$ and X, Y and Z have a value of $\cdot$FALSE$\cdot$, what are the values of the following expressions?

1. A $\cdot$AND$\cdot$ $\cdot$NOT$\cdot$ $(B$ $\cdot$OR$\cdot$ C $\cdot$OR$\cdot$ $X)$

2. $\cdot$NOT$\cdot$ X $\cdot$OR$\cdot$ Y $\cdot$AND$\cdot$ A

3. X $\cdot$OR$\cdot$ $(B$ $\cdot$AND$\cdot$ X $\cdot$OR$\cdot$ $C)$

ANSWERS

1. ·FALSE·
2. ·TRUE·
3. ·TRUE·

EXAMPLE

The Staff at International Egg Timers have been asked the following
six questions which they can answer either YES or NO.

1. Do you like eggs?
2. Is egg beating cruel?
3. Are your hard-boiled?
4. Is happiness egg shaped?
5. Can you count up to three?
6. Are eggs square?

We want to find and print out the names of anyone who has answered
YES to questions 1 and 4 and NO to all the others.

A punched card is prepared with the following information:

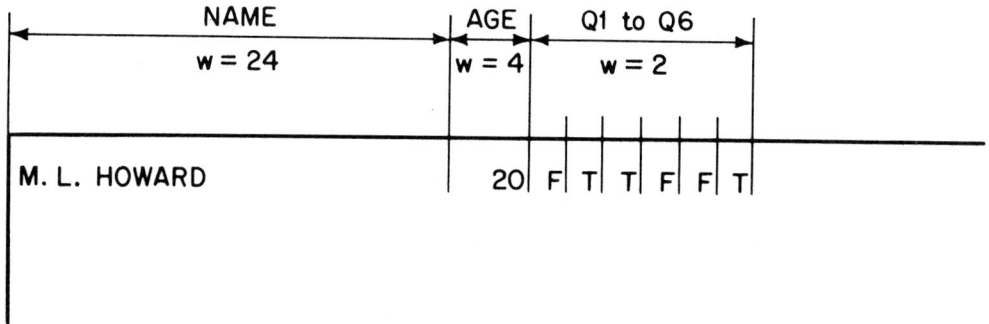

If the answer to a question is YES a T is punched in the appropriate column. If the answer is NO an F is punched.

The end of data is marked by a card on which the age is 999.

In the program we want a six element logical array to hold the answers to the questions.

C	STATEMENT NUMBER	CONT.		FC
1 2 3 4 5	6	7 8 9 10 11 12 13 14 15 16 17 18 19 20 21 22 23 24 25 26 27 28 29 30 31 32 33 34 35
		MASTER CENSUS
		LOGICAL Q(6)

Also, we want a three element array to hold the person's name. We could, of course, define the array using a Dimension Statement but there is no reason why we should not use the Logical Statement,

C	STATEMENT NUMBER	CONT.		FOR
1 2 3 4 5	6	7 8 9 10 11 12 13 14 15 16 17 18 19 20 21 22 23 24 25 26 27 28 29 30 31 32 33 34 35 36
		MASTER CENSUS
		LOGICAL Q(6), NAME(3)

and if we put the age into the variable AGE we must define it as Integer.

C	STATEMENT NUMBER	CONT.		FOR
1 2 3 4 5	6	7 8 9 10 11 12 13 14 15 16 17 18 19 20 21 22 23 24 25 26 27 28 29 30 31 32 33 34 35 36
		MASTER CENSUS
		LOGICAL Q(6), NAME(3)
		INTEGER AGE

Before turning over, try writing the statements to read a card and to test for the end of data.

ANSWER

C	STATEMENT NUMBER	CONT.	FORTRAN
	1 2 3 4 5	6	7 8 9 10 11 12 13 14 15 16 17 18 19 20 21 22 23 24 25 26 27 28 29 30 31 32 33 34 35 36 37 38
			MASTER CENSUS
			LOGICAL Q(6), NAME(3)
			INTEGER AGE
	51		FORMAT (3A8, IA, 6L2)
			READ (50, 51) (NAME (I), I=1,3),
		2	AGE, (Q(J), J=1,6)
			IF (999-AGE) 99, 99, 0

Continuation Lines

Notice that we have continued the Read Statement on to a second line.

In Fortran a Statement can have as many as nineteen continuation lines.

Column 6 of the initial line of the Statement must be blank or contain the number 0.

Column 6 of the continuation lines may contain any character other than a blank or a zero.

260

We are looking for people who have answered YES to questions 1 and 4 and NO to questions 2, 3, 5 and 6.

That is we want to find cards where:

Q (1) ·AND· Q (4)
is ·TRUE·

and

Q (2) ·OR· Q (3) ·OR· Q (5) ·OR· Q (6)
is ·FALSE·

We could combine these into one large Logical expression and test if it were ·TRUE· or ·FALSE· but this would make for a rather cumbersome Logical IF Statement.

So, set each of these expressions to equal a Logical variable and then complete the program.

ANSWER

C	STATEMENT NUMBER	CONT.	FORTRAN S
			MASTER CENSUS
			LOGICAL Q(6), NAME(3), R, S
			INTEGER AGE
51			FORMAT (3A8, I4, 6L2)
89			READ (50, 51) (NAME(I), I=1,4),
		2	AGE, (Q(J), J=1,6)
			IF (999-AGE) 99, 99, 0
			R = Q(1) .AND. Q(4)
			S = Q(2).OR.Q(3).OR.Q(5).OR.Q(6)
			IF (R .AND. .NOT. S) WRITE (60, 61)
		2	(NAME(I), I=1,3)
61			FORMAT (20X, 3A8)
			GO TO 89
99			STOP
			END
			FINISH

Did you remember to declare the mode of the two additional Logical Variables?

Logical Relational Expressions

Another kind of expression which has a value of ·TRUE· or ·FALSE· is the Logical Relational Expression.

It is formed between two arithmetic expressions and one of the following Relational Operators:

·LT· less than

·LE· less than or equal to

·EQ· equal to

·NE· not equal to

·GT· greater than

·GE· greater than or equal to

Again the full stops are an essential part of the operator.

EXAMPLE

Although the Logical Relational expression does not offer any new facilities it does provide a neat and short way of examining data.

A simple and obvious use of the Relational expression is in testing for the end of data.

We could for example replace the Arithmetic IF Statement in the last example

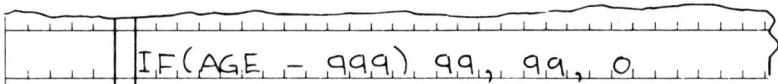

by a Logical IF Statement

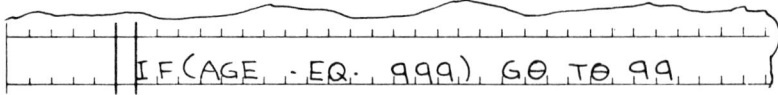

EXAMPLE

A bolt manufacturer makes a range of bolts in 8 diameters, from $\frac{1}{8}$ inch diameter to 1 inch diameter. Each bolt is identified by a four-figure part number, the first digit of which gives the bolt diameter. 1*XXX* is $\frac{1}{8}$ inch diameter, 2*XXX* is $\frac{1}{4}$ inch diameter and so on in $\frac{1}{8}$ inch increments.

Each sales transaction is punched on a card as follows:

PARTNO	QUANT	Date			NAME
w = 5	w = 8	w = 3	w = 3	w = 3	w = 32
1200	25600	09	09	67	

We have been asked to write a program which will discover the name of any customer who has bought $\frac{1}{2}$ inch bolts in the period July to September 1966 inc. and print out his name and the quantity sold.

Write the coding necessary to read in a card and test for the end of data. The end of data is marked by a card with the Part number 9999 on it.

Make provision in the coding for two Logical variables DATE and DIA.

ANSWER

C	STATEMENT NUMBER	CONT.	FORTRAN ST
			MASTER BOLT
			INTEGER PARTNO, QUANT, DAY, MONTH,
		1	YEAR, NAME(4)
			LOGICAL DATE, DIA
	51		FORMAT (I5, I8, 3I3, 4A8)
			READ (50, 51) PARTNO, QUANT, DAY,
		1	MONTH, YEAR, (NAME(I), I=1,4)
			IF (PARTNO .EQ. 9999) GO TO 99

We want to find cards for transactions which took place between July and September.

So, we want MONTH to be greater than or equal to 7:

MONTH ·GE· 7

and MONTH to be less than or equal to 9.

MONTH ·LE· 9

The Logical operators, ·NOT·, ·AND·, ·OR·, can be used to join any expression which has a value of ·TRUE· or ·FALSE·.

So, we can join the two Relational expressions with a Logical ·AND·.

MONTH ·GE· 7 ·AND· MONTH ·LE· 9

In the Statement:

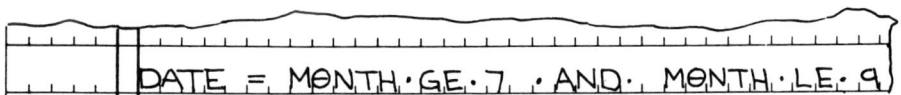

the Logical variable DATE will only have a value of ·TRUE· if both the Relational Expressions are ·TRUE·.

Order of Evaluation

Within a complete Logical expression the order of evaluation is:

RELATIONAL EXPRESSIONS
FUNCTION REFERENCES
LOGICAL EXPRESSIONS IN BRACKETS
·NOT·
·AND·
·OR·

1. Write the statement which will give the logical variable DIA a value of ·TRUE· if PARTNO is in the range 4*XXX*.

2. Test the value of DATE and DIA and act accordingly.

Then finish the program.

ANSWER

C	STATEMENT NUMBER	CONT.	FORTRAN STATEMENT
			MASTER BOLT
			INTEGER PARTNO, QUANT, DAY, MONTH
		1	YEAR, NAME(4)
			LOGICAL DATE, DIA
	51		FORMAT(I5, I8, 3I3, 4A8)
	89		READ(50, 51) PARTNO, QUANT, DAY,
		1	MONTH, YEAR, (NAME(I), I=1,4)
			IF(PARTNO .EQ. 9999) GO TO 99
			DATE = MONTH.GE.7 .AND. MONTH.LE.9
			DIA=PARTNO.GE.4000. AND. PARTNO.LT.5000
			IF(DATE .AND. DIA)WRITE(60, 61)
		1	(NAME(I), I=1,4), QUANT
	61		FORMAT(20X, 4A8, 10X, I8)
			GO TO 89
	99		STOP
			END
			FINISH

270

A reminder:

Logical Operators can only be used to join expressions which have Logical values. So, it is quite wrong to say, for example:

PARTNO ·GE· 4000 ·AND· ·LT· 5000

Since ·LT· 5000 is not a valid Relational expression.

The Computed GO TO Statement

A useful control statement we've not yet used is the COMPUTED GO TO Statement, which transfers control to one of a number of statements depending on the value of an Integer variable.

For example:

In a program the variable PRICE contains the price of an article in pennies and the Integer variable I contains a district number 1, 2, 3 or 4.

Customers get a discount depending on the district they live in.

$$
\begin{aligned}
\text{District } 1 &= 15\% \text{ discount} \\
2 &= 10\% \\
3 &= 5\% \\
4 &= 0\%
\end{aligned}
$$

Here is the coding for each of the discounts:

```
26    PRICE = PRICE - PRICE*15/100
      GO TO 77
27    PRICE = PRICE - PRICE*10/100
      GO TO 77
28    PRICE = PRICE - PRICE*5/100
77    TOTAL = PRICE * QUANT
```

All that is needed is a Control Statement which will:

GO TO 26 when $I = 1$
GO TO 27 when $I = 2$
GO TO 28 when $I = 3$
GO TO 77 when $I = 4$

In Fortran this can be written as one Computed GO TO Statement:

```
      GO TO (26, 27, 28, 77), I
26    PRICE = PRICE - PRICE*15/100
      GO TO 77
27    PRICE = PRICE - PRICE*10/100
      GO TO 77
28    PRICE = PRICE - PRICE*5/100
77    TOTAL = PRICE * QUANT
```

The Computed GO TO Statement has the general form:

GO TO (k_1, k_2, k_3, - - - - kn), I

k_1, k_2, k_3, - - - - kn are the Statement Numbers of executable statements in the same segment as the computed GO TO Statement.

I is an Integer variable in the range 1 to n.

When I has a value of 1, k_1 is executed.

When I has a value of 2, k_2 is executed.

When I has a value of n, k_n is executed.

EXAMPLE

If I has a value of 4, then in the statement:

GO TO (21, 22, 32, 36, 99), I

The computer will go to statement labelled 36.

As with the arithmetic IF Statement any of the statement numbers k_1, k_2, k_3, etc., can be labelled 0. If this is the statement to be executed then the computer will proceed to the next executable statement.

The Integer I must be in the range 1 to n.

For example, it is an error for I to have a value of 0.

Program Segmentation

One of the reasons for writing a routine as a Function Segment is that it is required more than once in a program.

There are many advantages in dividing a program up into segments each of which is perhaps called only once.

These can be listed as:

1. A program divided into segments which reflect the logic of the program is easier to write—and easier to understand.

2. Each segment can be written and tested independently. An error occurring in one segment does not mean that the whole program has to be altered.

3. A routine written as a segment of a program can easily be adapted for another program.

4. Shorter segments lead to shorter compilation time.

Function Segments

The mode of a Function Segment can either be given by the initial letter of the Function's name or in the Function Statement. For example:

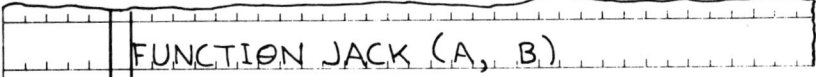

is an Integer Function, and:

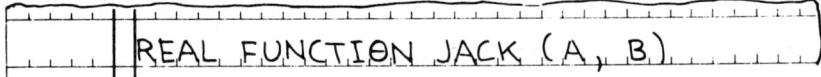

is a Real Function.

So far we have only dealt with Integer and Real Functions, but a Function Segment can be Integer, Real, Double Precision, Complex or Logical. For all but Integer and Real Function we must, of course, give the mode in the Function Statement.

For example:

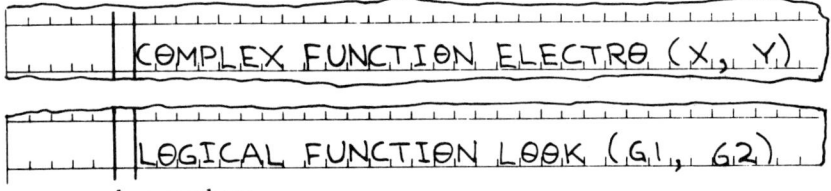

and remember:

If the mode of a Function Segment is not given by its initial letter, the Function name must appear in an appropriate Type Statement in any segment in which it is used.

277

Function Segment Arguments

The arguments of a Function Segment are dummy variables used only to define the segment. They are not related to variables of the same name in any other segment.

The dummy variables must agree in number and in mode with the variables which will replace them.

The mode of a dummy variable is given by its initial letter or by a Type Statement in the Function Segment.

EXAMPLE

The problem is to write a program which will find out the day of the week of any date between 1st January 1800 and 31st December 1999.

The method is given on the next page.

The input data is on cards.

DAY MONTH YEAR

w = 3	w = 3	w = 5	
15	8	1915	

and to mark the end of data we have a card on which the Year is 9999.

Output will take one of the three forms:

24 12 1966 IS A TUESDAY

32   9 1948 IS NON EXISTENT

12   1 1789 IS OUT OF RANGE

A Formula to find the day of the week

Here is a method of finding the day of the week of any date between 1st January 1800 and 31st December 1999.

What day of the week was August 27th, 1815?

1. Take the last two digits of the year   15

2. Add a quarter of this, neglecting remainder   +3

3. Add the date of the month   +27

4. For January add 1 (if leap year add 0)
   For February add 4 (if leap year add 3)
   For March add 4
   For April add 0
   For May add 2
   For June add 5
   For July add 0
   For August add 3   +3
   For September add 6
   For October add 1
   For November add 4
   For December add 6

5. For 19th Century add 2   +2
   For 20th Century add 0

                                          —
                                         50
                                          —

6. Divide by 7, and the remainder gives the day of the week:

$$50 \div 7 \quad \text{Remainder } 1$$

Sunday 1, Monday 2, Tuesday 3, Wednesday 4, Thursday 5, Friday 6, Saturday 0.

August 27th, 1815, was a Sunday.

To simplify the coding of this program we shall divide it into four segments.

1. The Master Segment (call it GRUNDY)

   The Master Segment will input and output data and control the other segments.

2. INTEGER FUNCTION REM

   This does the arithmetic calculations to find the remainder.

3. LOGICAL FUNCTION GEN

   This tests for dates which are non existent.

4. LOGICAL FUNCTION LEAP

   This tests if a year is a leap year.

Here is a general flowchart for the problem.

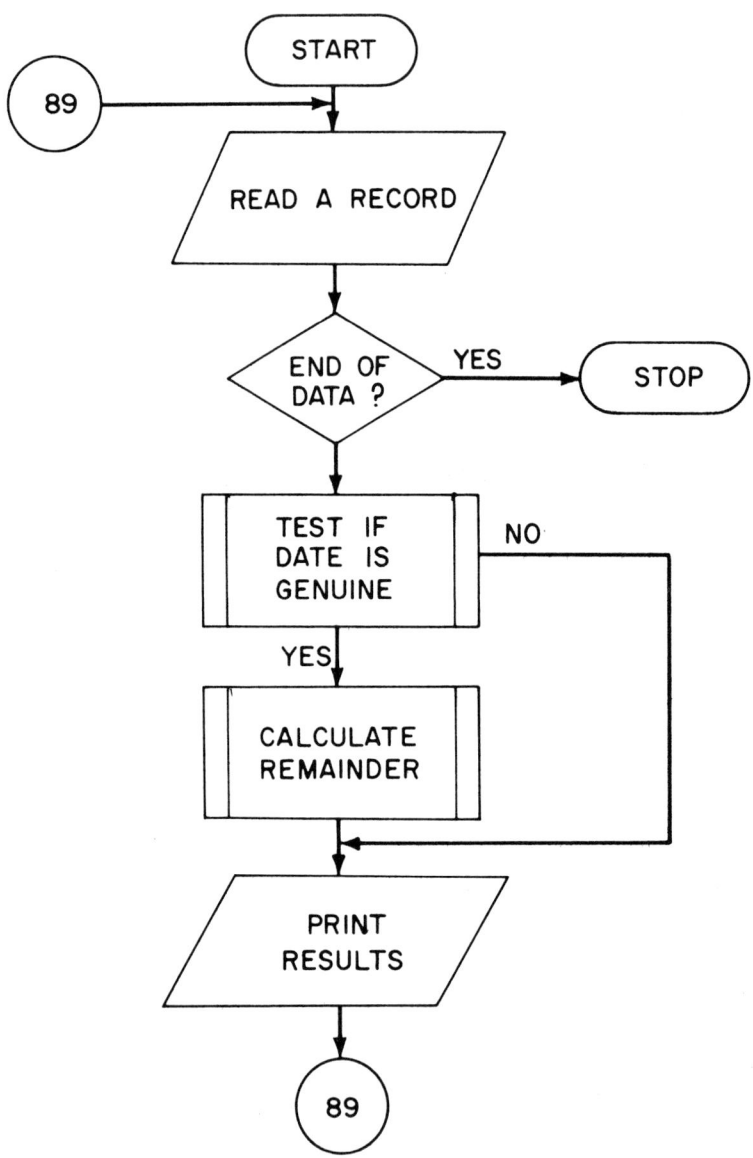

QUESTION

Start by drawing a flowchart for the segment to test for leap years.

Draw it as you would a complete program but replace the STOP box by a RETURN box.

A leap year is one which is divisible by four. If it is a century it must be divisible by 400.

ANSWER

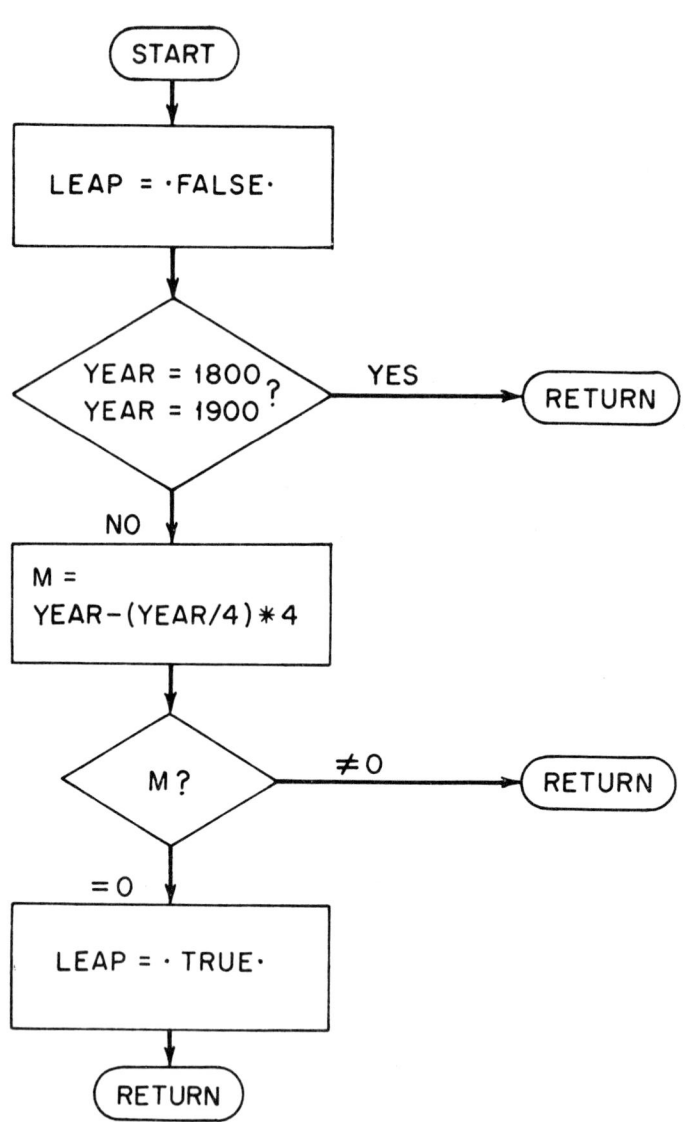

QUESTION

We can code this segment straight away. The only thing we need to know is that the variables DAY, MONTH and YEAR are Integer and consequently the dummy variable in the Function segment definition must also be Integer.

C	STATEMENT NUMBER	CONT.		FC
1 2 3 4 5	6	7 8 9 10 11 12 13 14 15 16 17 18 19 20 21 22 23 24 25 26 27 28 29 30 31 32 33 34 35		
		LOGICAL FUNCTION LEAP (YEAR)		
		INTEGER YEAR		

Try to complete the coding for this segment before turning over.

ANSWER

C	STATEMENT NUMBER	CONT.	FORTRAN STA
			LOGICAL FUNCTION LEAP(YEAR)
			INTEGER YEAR
			LEAP = .FALSE.
			IF(YEAR.EQ.1800 .OR. YEAR.EQ.1900)
	2		GO TO 3
			IF(MOD(YEAR, 4)) 3, 0, 3
			LEAP = .TRUE.
3			RETURN
			END

The standard function MOD gives the remainder of Integer division.

For example:

If the year were 1967 then MOD (YEAR, 4) would give the result:

$$\text{YEAR} - (\text{YEAR}/4)*4$$
$$= 1967 \quad - (1967/4)*4$$
$$= 1967 \quad - (491)*4$$
$$= 1967 \quad - 1964$$
$$= 3$$

QUESTION

Draw a flowchart for a segment to test if the date is genuine. Assume that years which are out of range have already been discovered.

Compare your flowchart with the one shown overleaf and then code the segment. Again we will have to declare the mode of any variables or Function Segments we use.

C	STATEMENT NUMBER	CONT.	FORTRAN STATEMENT
			LOGICAL FUNCTION GEN (DAY, MONTH, YEAR)
			INTEGER DAY, MONTH, YEAR
			LOGICAL LEAP

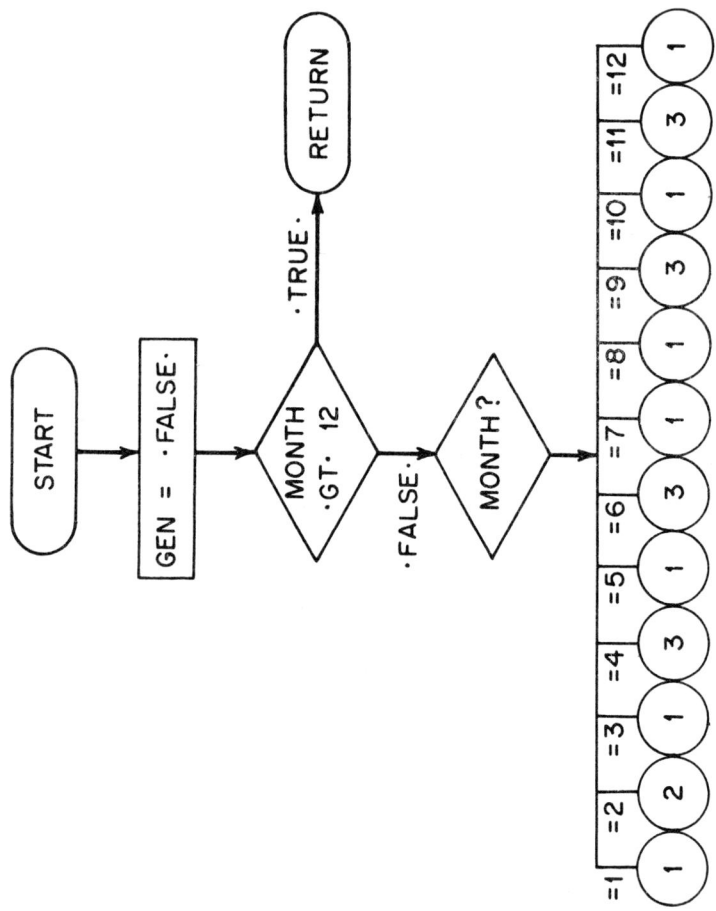

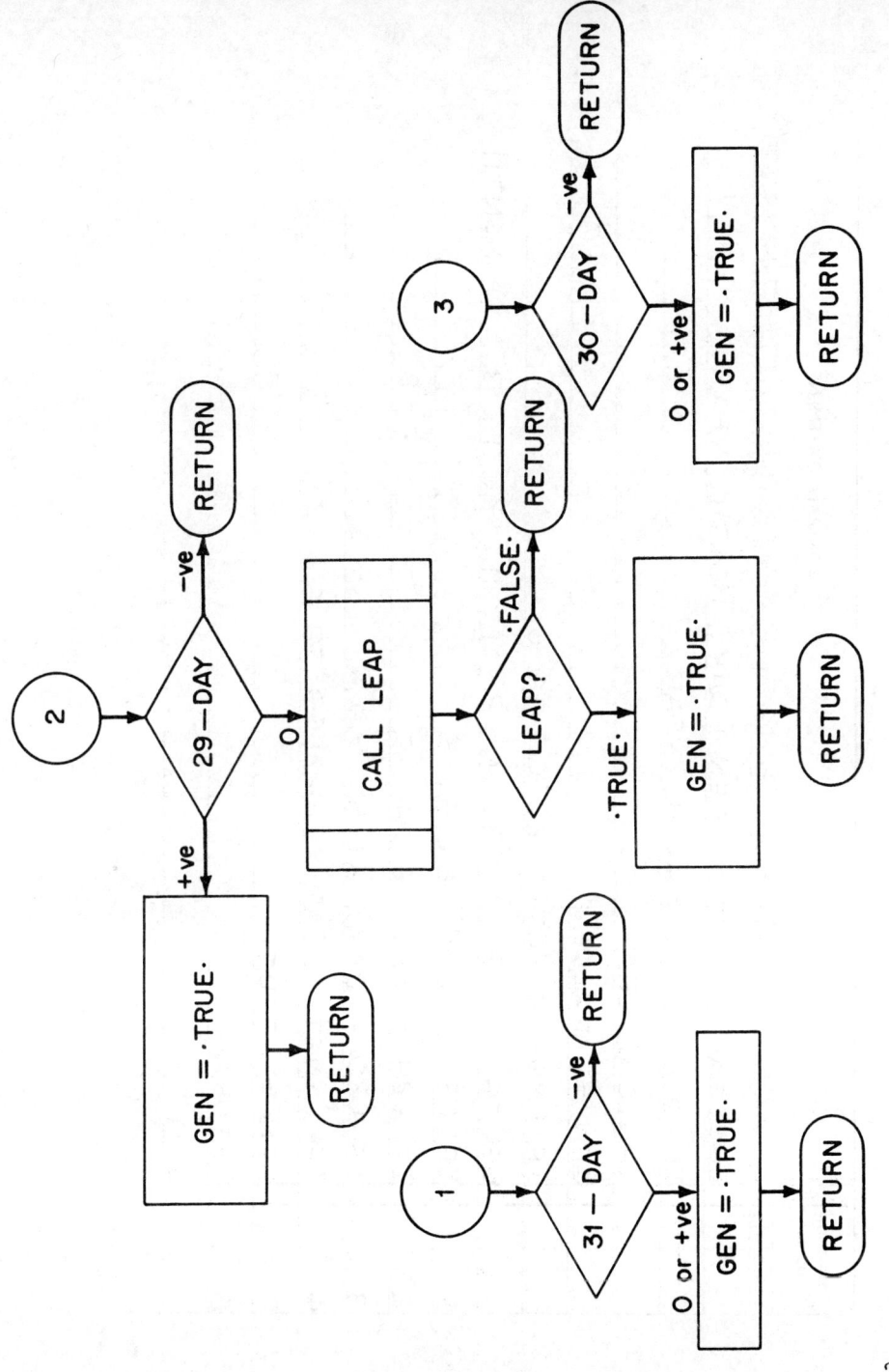

289

ANSWER

C	STATEMENT NUMBER	CONT	FORTRAN STATEMENT
			LOGICAL FUNCTION GEN (DAY, MONTH, YEAR)
			INTEGER DAY, MONTH, YEAR
			LOGICAL LEAP
			GEN = .FALSE.
			IF (MONTH .GT. 12) GO TO 6
			GO TO (1, 2, 1, 3, 1, 3, 1, 1, 3, 1, 3, 1), MONTH
	1		IF (31 - DAY) 6, 5, 5
	2		IF (29 - DAY) 6, 4, 5
	3		IF (30 - DAY) 6, 5, 5
	4		IF (.NOT. LEAP(YEAR)) GO TO 6
	5		GEN = .TRUE.
	6		RETURN
			END

QUESTION

Now all that remains is to write the program.

Draw flowcharts for the Master Segment and for the segment to compute the remainder.

Compare them with the flowcharts shown on the next four pages and then write the coding.

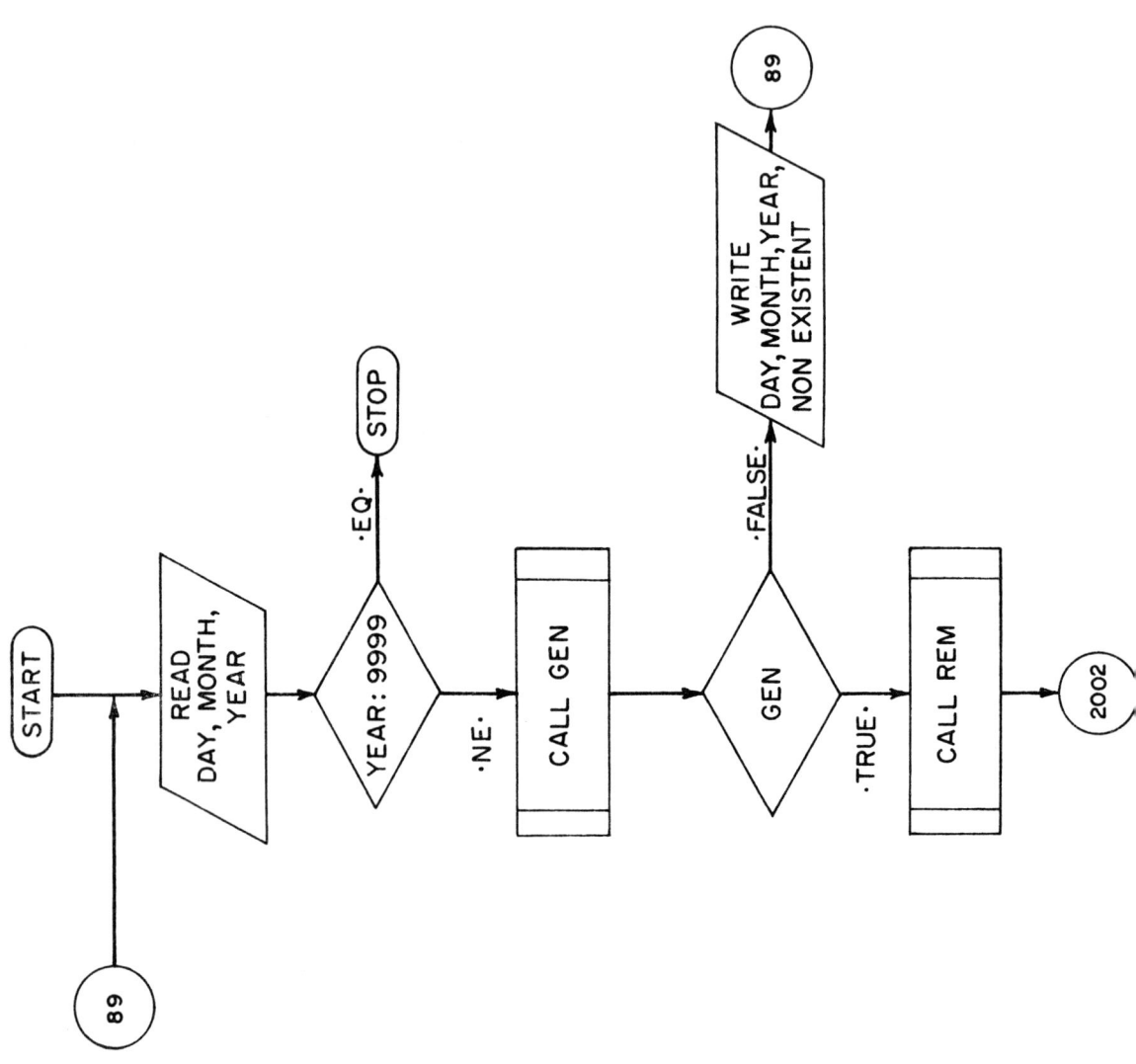

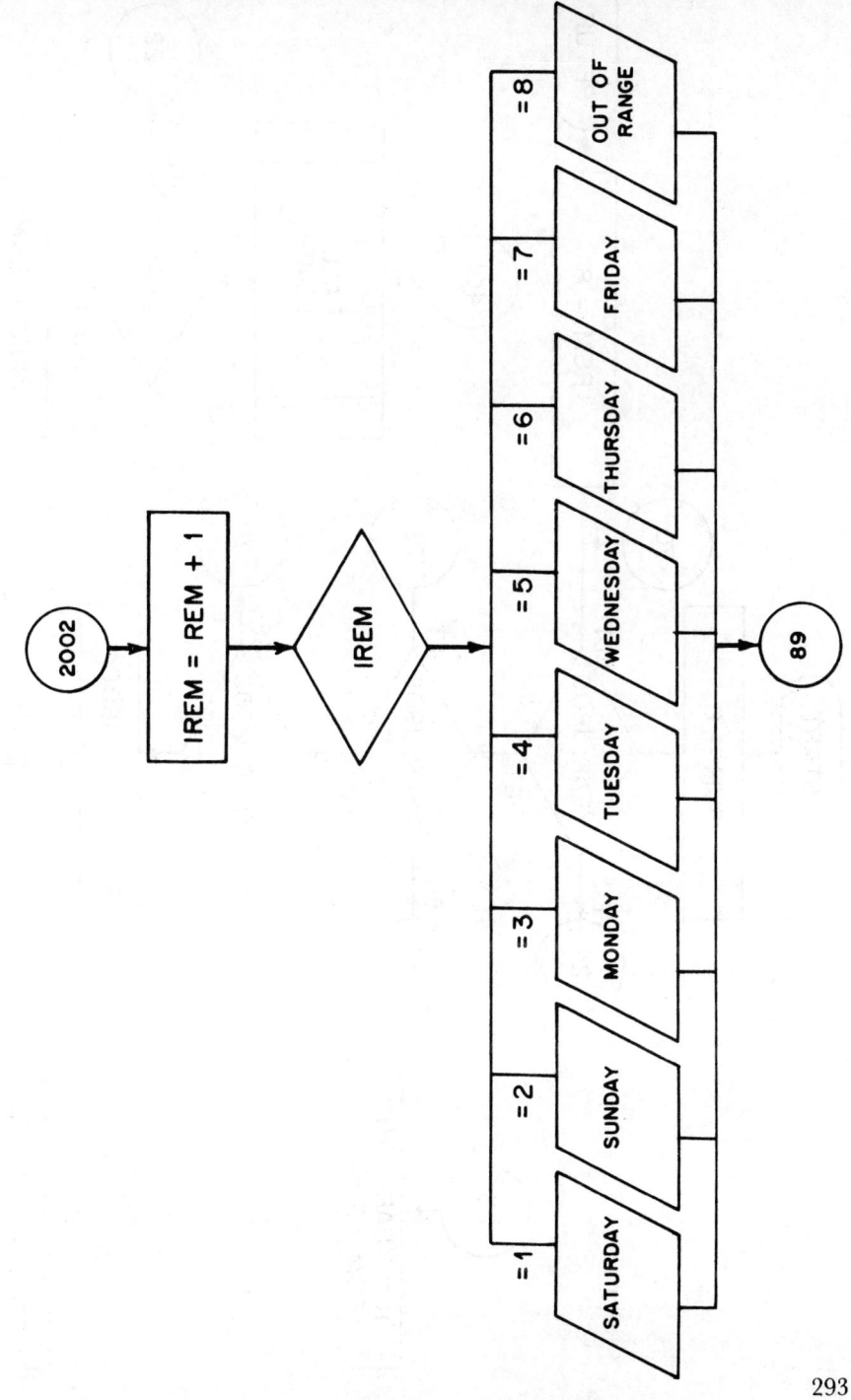

293

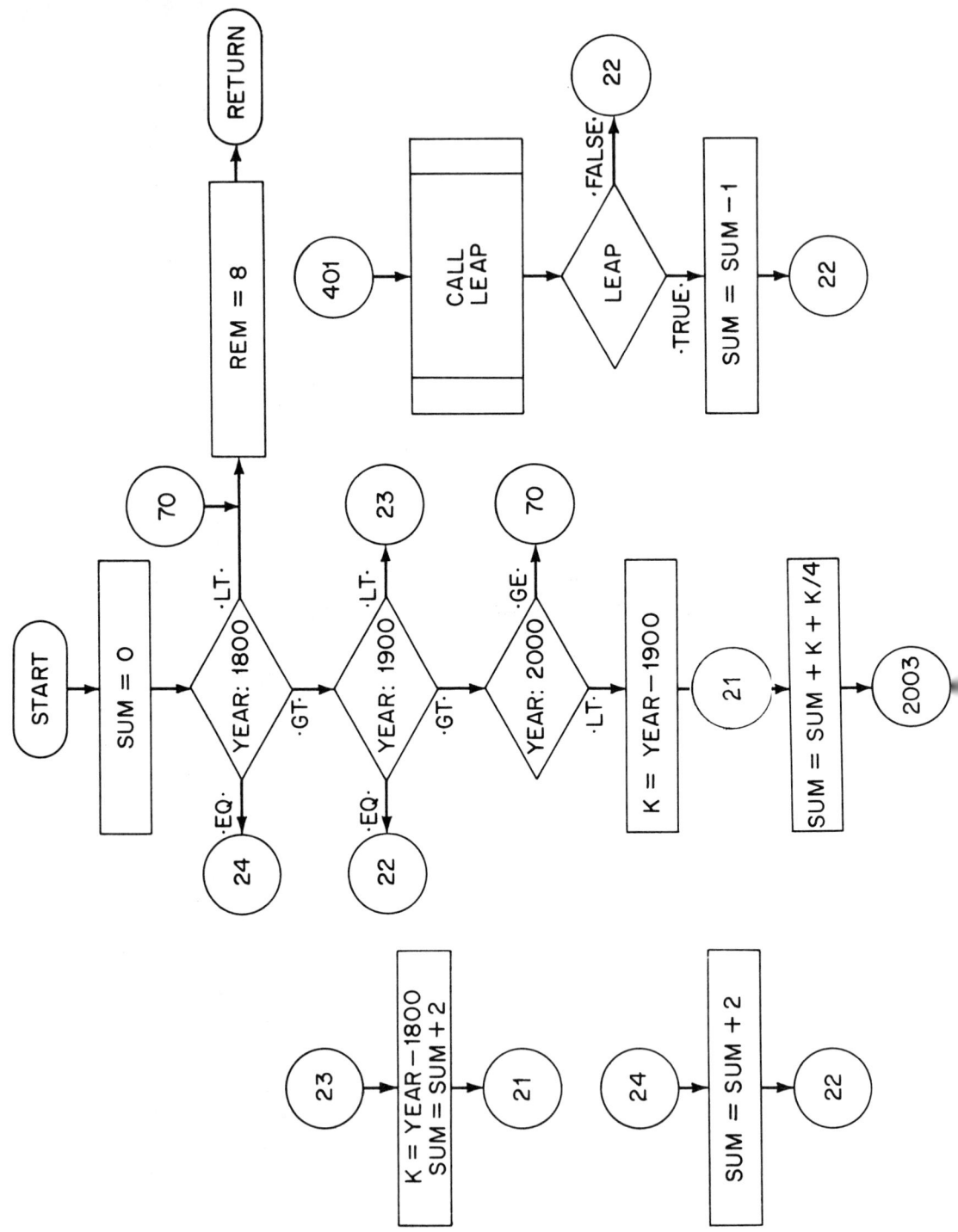

294

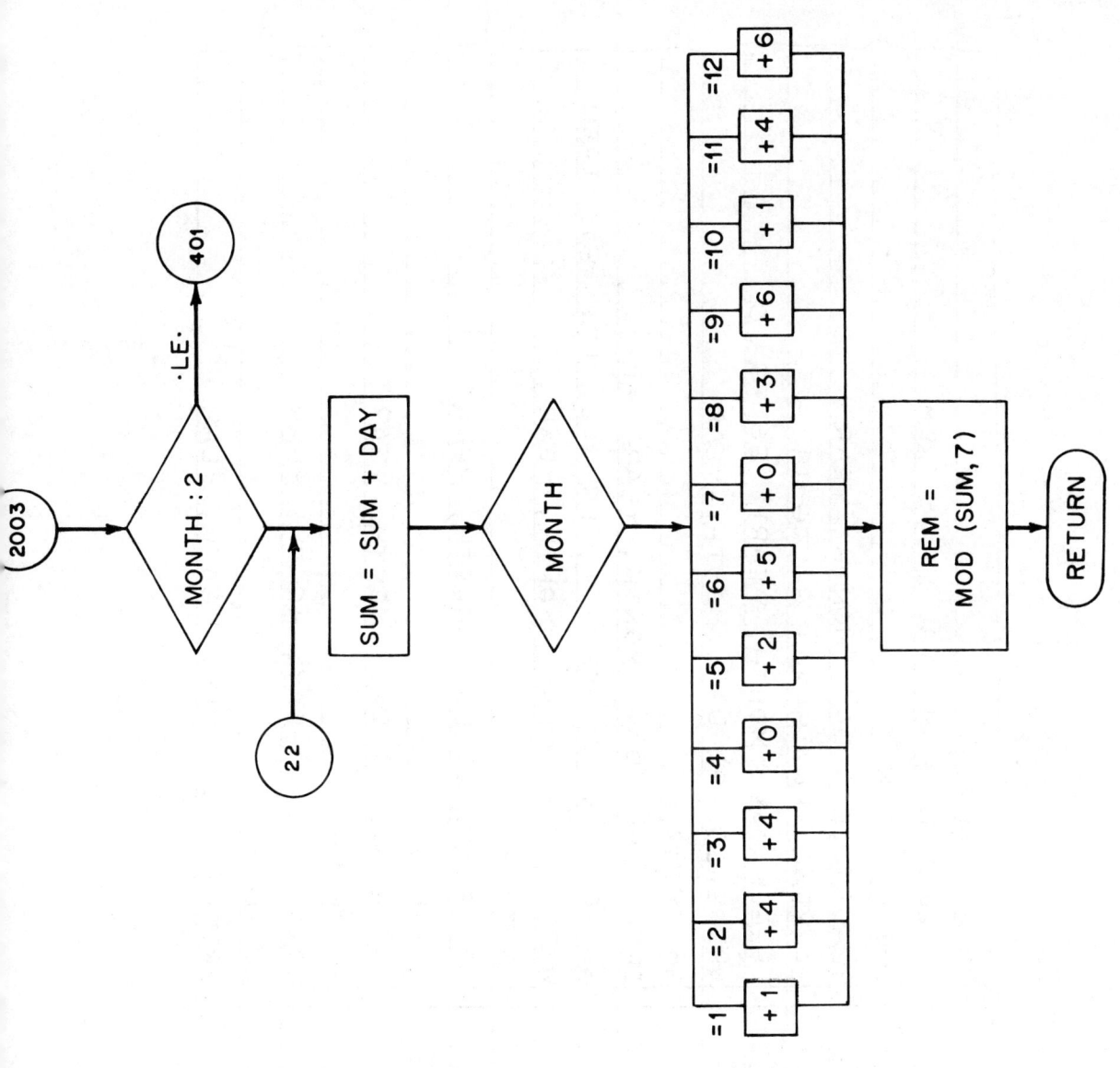

```
       MASTER GRUNDY
       INTEGER DAY, MONTH, YEAR, REM
       LOGICAL GEN
89     READ(50,51) DAY, MONTH, YEAR
       IF(YEAR .EQ. 9999) GO TO 99
       IF(GEN(DAY, MONTH, YEAR)) GO TO 10
       WRITE(60,69) DAY, MONTH, YEAR
       GO TO 89
10     IREM = REM(DAY, MONTH, YEAR) +1
       GO TO (11, 12, 13, 14, 15, 16, 17, 18), IREM
11     WRITE(60,61) DAY, MONTH, YEAR
       GO TO 89
12     WRITE(60,62) DAY, MONTH, YEAR
       GO TO 89
13     WRITE(60,63) DAY, MONTH, YEAR
       GO TO 89
14     WRITE(60,64) DAY, MONTH, YEAR
       GO TO 89
15     WRITE(60,65) DAY, MONTH, YEAR
```

```
        GO TO 89
 16     WRITE(60,66) DAY, MONTH, YEAR
        GO TO 89
 17     WRITE(60,67) DAY, MONTH, YEAR
        GO TO 89
 18     WRITE(60,68) DAY, MONTH, YEAR
        GO TO 89
 61     FORMAT(2I4, I6, 16H IS A SATURDAY )
 62     FORMAT(2I4, I6, 16H IS A SUNDAY )
 63     FORMAT(2I4, I6, 16H IS A MONDAY )
 64     FORMAT(2I4, I6, 16H IS A TUESDAY )
 65     FORMAT(2I4, I6, 16H IS A WEDNESDAY)
 66     FORMAT(2I4, I6, 16H IS A THURSDAY )
 67     FORMAT(2I4, I6, 16H IS A FRIDAY )
 68     FORMAT(2I4, I6, 17H IS OUT OF RANGE)
 69     FORMAT(2I4, I6, 17H IS NON EXISTENT)
 51     FORMAT(2I3, I5)
 99     STOP
        END
```

C	STATEMENT NUMBER	CONT.	FORTRAN STATEMENT
			INTEGER FUNCTION REM(DAY, MONTH, YEAR)
			INTEGER DAY, MONTH, YEAR, SUM
			LOGICAL LEAP
			SUM = 0
			IF (YEAR - 1800) 70, 24, 0
			IF (YEAR - 1900) 23, 22, 0
			IF (YEAR - 2000) 0, 70, 70
			K = YEAR - 1900
	21		SUM = SUM + K + K/4
			IF (MONTH .LE. 2 .AND. LEAP(YEAR)) SUM = SUM - 1
	22		SUM = SUM + DAY
			GO TO (1,4,4,0,2,5,0,3,6,1,4,6), MONTH
			GO TO 25
	1		SUM = SUM + 1
			GO TO 25
	2		SUM = SUM + 2
			GO TO 25

298

```
3    SUM = SUM + 3
     GO TO 25
4    SUM = SUM + 4
     GO TO 25
5    SUM = SUM + 5
     GO TO 25
6    SUM = SUM + 6
25   REM = MOD(SUM, 7)
     RETURN
23   K = YEAR - 1800
     SUM = SUM + 2
     GO TO 21
24   SUM = SUM + 2
     GO TO 22
10   REM = 7
     RETURN
```

Subroutines

A Function Segment is limited to producing one value and it must have at least one dummy argument.

A Subroutine Segment is another segment available in Fortran. It has none of the restrictions of the Function Segment. It is not limited to producing only one value; it can in fact set its results in arrays and there are no restrictions on the number of arguments it has.

Let's start off by writing a routine as a Function Segment and then rewriting it as a Subroutine.

EXAMPLE

We want to write a Function Segment which will compute the area of a triangle given the length of the three sides.

If the sides are a, b and c then

$$\text{area} = \sqrt{s(s-a)(s-b)(s-c)}$$

where $2s = a + b + c$.

We can write this in Fortran as:

```
S = (A + B + C)/2
AREA = SQRT (S *(S-A)*(S-B)*(S-C))
```

In a Function Segment, the name of the Function must be the same as the variable whose final value we want to be the value of the Function.

So, we must call this:

1	2	3	4	5	6	7 8 9 10 11 12 13 14 15 16 17 18 19 20 21 22 23 24 25 26 27 28 29 30 31 32 33 34 35 36 37 38 39 40
						FUNCTION AREA

In brackets after the Function name we list the dummy arguments of the Function. There must be at least one and in this case there are three, the lengths of the sides of the triangle A, B and C.

1	2	3	4	5	6	7 8 9 10 11 12 13 14 15 16 17 18 19 20 21 22 23 24 25 26 27 28 29 30 31 32 33 34 35 36 37 38 39 40
						FUNCTION AREA (A, B, C)
						S = (A + B + C)/2
						AREA = SQRT(S *(S-A)*(S-B)*(S-C))

We must have a Return Statement to return control to the calling segment and of course an END Statement.

1	2	3	4	5	6	7 8 9 10 11 12 13 14 15 16 17 18 19 20 21 22 23 24 25 26 27 28 29 30 31 32 33 34 35 36 37 38 39 40
						FUNCTION AREA (A, B, C)
						S = (A + B + C)/2
						AREA = SQRT(S *(S-A)*(S-B)*(S-C))
						RETURN
						END

303

When the Function Segment is used in the program it is simply a matter of replacing the dummy arguments by the actual arguments.

For example:

If in a program we wanted to sum the areas of two triangles whose sides were B, C, D and R, S, T we could use the Function Segment we have written by writing:

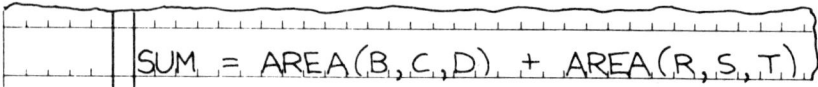

The actual arguments B and C have no relationship to the dummy arguments B and C in the Function Segment definition.

Now we shall write the same routine as a Subroutine Segment.

First we give the Subroutine a name.

A Subroutine name is used only to distinguish it from the other segments in the program. Consequently a Subroutine name has no mode significance and is subject to the same rules for names as a Master Segment.

Let's call this Subroutine TRING.

C	STATEMENT NUMBER	CONT.		F
1	2 3 4 5	6	7 8 9 10 11 12 13 14 15 16 17 18 19 20 21 22 23 24 25 26 27 28 29 30 31 32 33 34	
			SUBROUTINE TRING	

The dummy arguments of a Subroutine are used not only to supply the subroutine with values but also to return values to the segment which called it. That is, a Subroutine can be considered to have both input and output arguments.

In this subroutine we have three input arguments, the sides of the triangle, *A*, *B* and *C*, and one output argument the area of the triangle AREA.

We must list these in brackets after the subroutine name.

C	STATEMENT NUMBER	CONT.	FORTRAN
1 2 3 4 5		6	7 8 9 10 11 12 13 14 15 16 17 18 19 20 21 22 23 24 25 26 27 28 29 30 31 32 33 34 35 36 37 38
			SUBROUTINE TRING(A,B,C,AREA)
			S = (A + B + C)/2
			AREA = SQRT(S*(S-A)*(S-B)*(S-C))

As with the Function Segment we must have a Return Statement to return control to the calling segment and an End Statement.

C	STATEMENT NUMBER	CONT.	FORTRAN
1 2 3 4 5		6	7 8 9 10 11 12 13 14 15 16 17 18 19 20 21 22 23 24 25 26 27 28 29 30 31 32 33 34 35 36 37 38
			SUBROUTINE TRING(A,B,C,AREA)
			S = (A + B + C)/2
			AREA = SQRT(S*(S-A)*(S-B)*(S-C))
			RETURN
			END

306

The Call Statement

Unlike the Function Segment a Subroutine cannot be used simply by writing its name in a statement.

It must be introduced by a special statement, the Call Statement.

For example:

Let's say that again we want to sum the areas of the two triangles whose sides are B, C, D and R, S, T.

To find the area of the first triangle we call the subroutine by writing

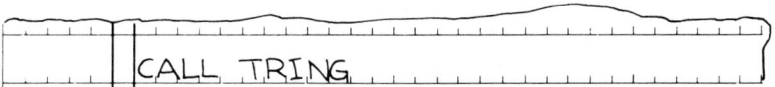

and then replace the dummy arguments by the actual arguments, B, C, D and the dummy argument AREA by the variable we want to hold the actual area of the triangle, AREA 1.

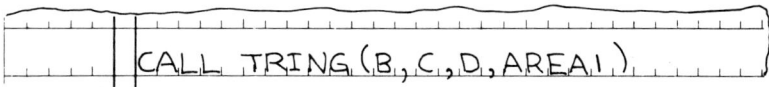

Try writing the Call Statement to find the area of the triangle R, S, T and put the value in AREA 2.

307

ANSWER

```
||CALL TRING (R, S, T, AREA2)
```

We now have:

```
||CALL TRING (B, C, D, AREA1)
||CALL TRING (R, S, T, AREA2)
```

We can now sum the areas by writing:

```
||CALL TRING (B, C, D, AREA1)
||CALL TRING (B, C, D, AREA2)
||SUM = AREA1 + AREA2
```

A Subroutine is not limited to returning only one value to the calling segment.

Say, for example, we want to write a subroutine for a coin analysis. That is one which will take a sum of money in pennies and find the minimum number of coins with which it can be composed.

The Subroutine is limited to the following coins:

> half crowns
> shillings
> sixpences
> pennies

In this Subroutine there is only one input argument, a number of pence; and four output arguments, the four types of coin.

Try writing the Subroutine before turning over.

ANSWER

C	STATEMENT NUMBER	CONT.	FORTRAN STATE
			SUBROUTINE MONEY (PENCE, H, S, X, D)
			INTEGER PENCE, H, S, X, D
			H = PENCE/30
			D = PENCE - H * 30
			S = D/12
			D = D - S * 12
			X = D/6
			D = D - X * 6
			RETURN
			END

QUESTION

This Master Segment uses the Subroutine we have just written. Insert the appropriate Call Statement.

C	STATEMENT NUMBER	CONT.	FORTRAN STATE
			MASTER CASH
			INTEGER INPENI, HAF, SHIL, SX, DEN
			READ (40, 41) INPENI
	→		
			WRITE (60, 61) HAF, SHIL, SX, DEN
			STOP
	41		FORMAT (I4)
	61		FORMAT (4I5)
			END

ANSWER

```
CALL MONEY (INPENI, HAF, SHIL, SX, DEN)
```

Subroutines with Arrays

Here is a routine to subtract a 30 element array *W* from a 30 element array *V*.

```
      DIMENSION U(30),V(30),W(30)
      DO 21 I = 1, 30
21    U(I) = V(I) - W(I)
```

To turn this into a Subroutine called **SUBT** we write:

```
      SUBROUTINE SUBT(U, V, W)
      DIMENSION U(30),V(30),W(30)
      DO 21 I = 1, 30
21    U(I) = V(I) - W(I)
      RETURN
      END
```

To call this Subroutine we write:

```
      CALL SUBT(A, B, C)
```

replacing the dummy array names with the real array names. These arrays must of course have been dimensioned in a previous statement.

313

Dynamic Dummy Arrays

The Subroutine shown could be used only to manipulate 30 element arrays.

In Fortran the size of the array can itself be a dummy variable. We could rewrite the previous example as

C	STATEMENT NUMBER	CONT.		F(
	1 2 3 4 5	6	7 8 9 10 11 12 13 14 15 16 17 18 19 20 21 22 23 24 25 26 27 28 29 30 31 32 33 34 35	
			SUBROUTINE SUBT (U, V, W, K)	
			DIMENSION U(K), V(K), W(K)	
			DO 21 I = 1, K	
	21		U(I) = V(I) - W(I)	
			RETURN	
			END	

Now each time the subroutine is called the array can be a different size.

For example:

		L = 50	
		CALL SUBT (A, B, C, L)	
		M = 100	
		CALL SUBT (E, F, G, M)	

QUESTION

1. Write a Subroutine to form a two dimensional array S, whose elements are the square of corresponding elements of an array T.

2. Using the Subroutine write the statements including Dimension statements, to form the squares of the array $A(40, 50)$ and the square of the array $B(20, 20)$.

ANSWER

1.

C	STATEMENT NUMBER	CONT.	FOR
1 2 3 4 5	6	7 8 9 10 11 12 13 14 15 16 17 18 19 20 21 22 23 24 25 26 27 28 29 30 31 32 33 34 35 36

```
      SUBROUTINE SQUARE (S,T,L,M)
      DIMENSION S(L,M),T(L,M)
      DO 21 I = 1, L
      DO 21 K = 1, M
21    S(I,J) = T(I,J) **2
      RETURN
      END
```

2.

```
      DIMENSION A(40,50),ASQ(40,50),
     2B(20,20),BSQ(20,20)
      K = 40
      L = 50
      CALL SQUARE(ASQ, A, K, L)
      M = 20
      CALL SQUARE(BSQ, B, M, M)
```

316

The Common Statement

When programs are compiled each segment is compiled independently. Consequently, they each occupy separate areas of core store. It follows from this that a value obtained in one segment is not immediately available in another.

In Fortran there are two ways of communicating values between segments:

1. By dummy arguments.

2. By specifying that certain areas of core store are COMMON to more than one segment.

For example

We want to write a program which reads 10 values from a card and punches them onto paper tape with a newline character between each value. To mark the end of the pack of cards we have a card with the value zero punched on it.

Let's say we have decided to write this as a Master Segment controlling an input Subroutine and an output Subroutine.

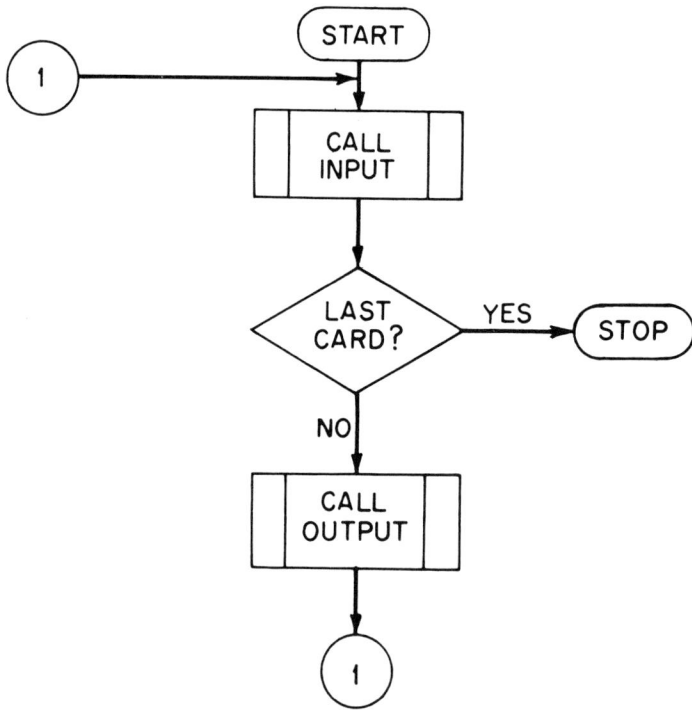

We want to read the card into an array which is common to all three segments.

Having decided to call the array LINK, there are three pieces of information we must give about this array in each segment it is used.

1. The mode of the array.

2. The Dimensions of the array (an array can be dimensioned in a Type, a Dimension or a Common Statement but it must be dimensioned once only in a segment).

3. That the array is Common.

C	STATEMENT NUMBER	CONT.		FC
	1 2 3 4 5 6	7 8 9 10 11 12 13 14 15 16 17 18 19 20 21 22 23 24 25 26 27 28 29 30 31 32 33 34 35	
		SUBROUTINE INPUT	
		REAL LINK	
		COMMON LINK(10)	
	51	FORMAT (10F8·3)	
		READ (50, 51) (LINK(I), I=1, 10)	
		RETURN	
		END	

Before turning over try writing the output Subroutine.

319

ANSWER

C	STATEMENT NUMBER	CONT.	FOR
			`SUBROUTINE OUTPUT`
			`REAL LINK`
			`COMMON LINK(10)`
	41		`FORMAT (F8.3)`
			`WRITE(40, 41)(LINK(I), I=1,10)`
			`RETURN`
			`END`

QUESTION

Now write the Master Segment to control the input and output
Subroutines.

ANSWER

C	STATEMENT NUMBER	CONT		FO
			MASTER RERITE	
			REAL LINK	
			COMMON LINK(10)	
89			CALL INPUT	
			IF(LINK(1)) 0, 99, 0	
			CALL OUTPUT	
			GO TO 89	
99			STOP	
			END	

Common Blocks

A program can have more than one area of store which is common between segments. Each area is called a Common Block and to distinguish between them each Common Block is given a name.

A Common Block Name follows the same rules as a Master Segment name. That is, it has no mode significance and bears no relationship to any variable of the same name in the program. A Common Block name must not be the same as that of a segment in the program or of a Standard Function. A Common Block name is written between oblique strokes.

For example:

A program consists of a Master Segment and two Subroutines. We want to make the variables A, B and C common to the Master Segment and one of the Subroutines and the variables W, X, Y and Z common to the Subroutines.

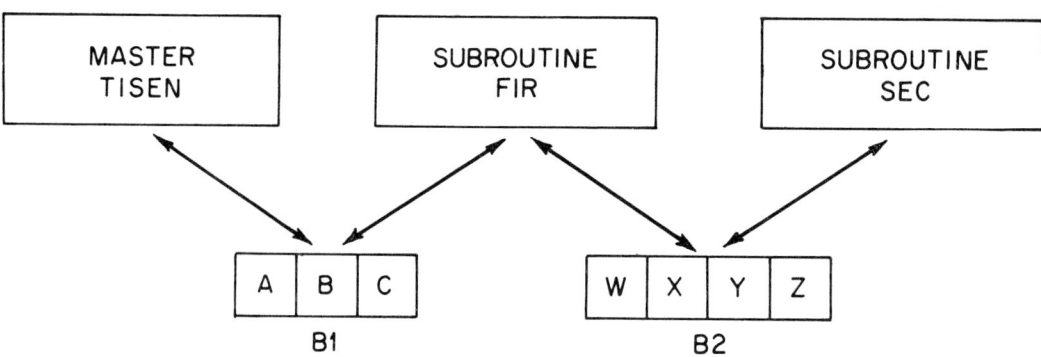

In the Master Segment we would write:

```
MASTER TISEN
COMMON /B1/ A,B,C
```

In the first Subroutine:

```
SUBROUTINE FIR
COMMON /B1/ A,B,C /B2/ W,X,Y,Z
```

and in the second Subroutine:

```
SUBROUTINE SEC
COMMON /B2/ W,X,Y,Z
```

If in the Master Segment we had written as before:

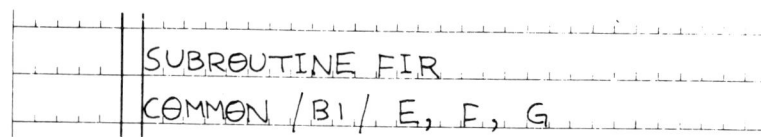

```
MASTER TISEN
COMMON /B1/ A, B, C
```

and in the first Subroutine:

```
SUBROUTINE FIR
COMMON /B1/ E, F, G
```

Then the variable A in the Master segment would occupy the same storage location as the variable E in the Subroutine, the variable B the same location as F and so on.

That is, variables are common by virtue of their position in the Common Block and not by name.

326

Arrays in Common Blocks

The elements of arrays are stored in Column order. That is, the left-hand subscript varies most rapidly.

For example:

The array $Z(2, 4)$ would be held as shown.

$Z(1, 1)$ $Z(2, 1)$ $Z(3, 1)$ $Z(4, 1)$ $Z(1, 2)$ $Z(2, 2)$ $Z(3, 3)$ $Z(4, 4)$

Two arrays in common need not have the same dimensions. In one segment we could say:

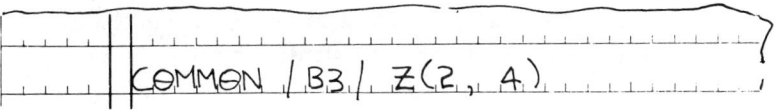

and in another:

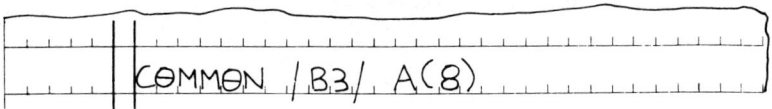

You must of course remember the order in which arrays are stored if you declare two arrays with different dimensions to be Common.

Blank Common Block

In every Program you are allowed one Common Block with no name.

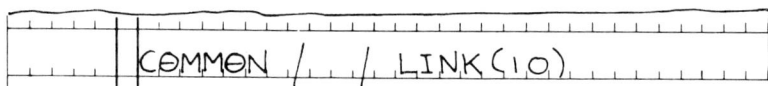

This is called the Blank Common Block. When the Blank Common Block is the first Common Block specified in a Common Statement then the two oblique strokes can be omitted.

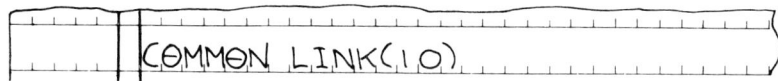

You will see that the Common array LINK in the first program was in fact in the Blank Common Block.

328

QUESTION

A program consists of a Master Segment and two Subroutines.

Write the Common Statement for each of the segments to declare:

(a) a 10 × 10 array common to every segment,

(b) four variables A, B, C, D common to each of the Subroutines.

ANSWER

C	STATEMENT NUMBER	CONT.	FORTRAN STA
1 2 3 4 5	6	7 8 9 10 11 12 13 14 15 16 17 18 19 20 21 22 23 24 25 26 27 28 29 30 31 32 33 34 35 36 37 38 39 40	
		MASTER PIC	
		COMMON /B1/ Z(10,10)	

		SUBROUTINE A1
		COMMON /B1/ Z(10,10) /B2/ A,B,C,D

		SUBROUTINE A2
		COMMON /B1/ Z(10,10) /B2/ A,B,C,D

330

The Data Statement

You have used the executable Arithmetic Statement to give initial values to variables and array elements:

```
PI = 3.14159
K(1) = 1
K(2) = 7
```

A Data Statement is a non-executable statement used to give initial values to variables and array elements.

First of all we write:

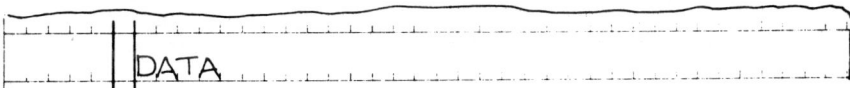

and follow it with the list of variables and array elements:

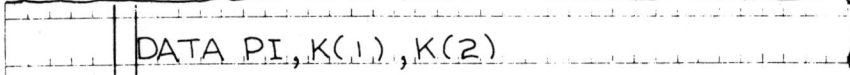

and then the corresponding list of values:

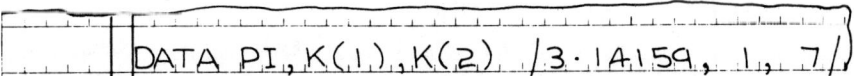

If we had a further list of initial values for variables, say:

$$CV = \cdot 17$$
$$CP = \cdot 24$$

we could extend the existing Data Statement:

```
0 DATA PI,K(1),K(2) /3·14159, 1, 7/,
1 CV,CP /·17, ·24/
```

that is we could extend the Data Statement by writing another list of variables followed by its corresponding list of values.

If we had a further value, say:

$$\text{BOOL} = \cdot \text{TRUE} \cdot$$

we could again extend the statement:

```
0 DATA PI,K(1),K(2) /3·14159, 1, 7/,
1 CV,CP /·17, ·24/, BOOL /·TRUE·/
```

The Data Statement

Here is the general form of the Data Statement:

$$\textbf{DATA } \mathbf{R_1/d_1/, \ R_2/d_2/, \ R_3/d_3/}$$

$\mathbf{R_1, \ R_2}$ etc. are lists of variables and array elements.

The list must not include the dummy arguments of Function Segments or Subroutines.

The Subscripts of array elements must be unsigned Integer Constants.

$\mathbf{d_1, \ d_2}$ etc. are the corresponding list of values.
Note that each list is separated by a comma.

Multiple Assignment

To give the same value to more than one variable we have used the executable Multiple Assignment Statement:

```
A, B, C = 0
```

The equivalent non-executable Data Statement is:

```
DATA A,B,C /3*0/
```

If we also had:

```
X, Y = 9.9
```

We could have written:

```
DATA A,B,C,X,Y /3*0, 2*9.9/
```

or, of course:

```
DATA A,B,C /3*0/, X,Y /2*9.9/
```

That is we give the number of times a value is repeated followed by *.

QUESTION

1. Here is a list of initial values for variables:

$$G = 1{\cdot}4$$
$$R = 53{\cdot}5$$

Write the corresponding Data Statement.

Extend the statement to include:

$$\text{ISO} = {\cdot}\text{TRUE}{\cdot}$$

Further extend the statement to include:

$$T(1) = 49{\cdot}0$$
$$T(2) = 153{\cdot}0$$

2. Write the equivalent Data Statement in a single block:

$$I, J, K, L = 1$$
$$A, B = 1{\cdot}0$$
$$X = 99$$

Extend the Statement to give a value of ${\cdot}999$ to E, F, G.

ANSWER

1.

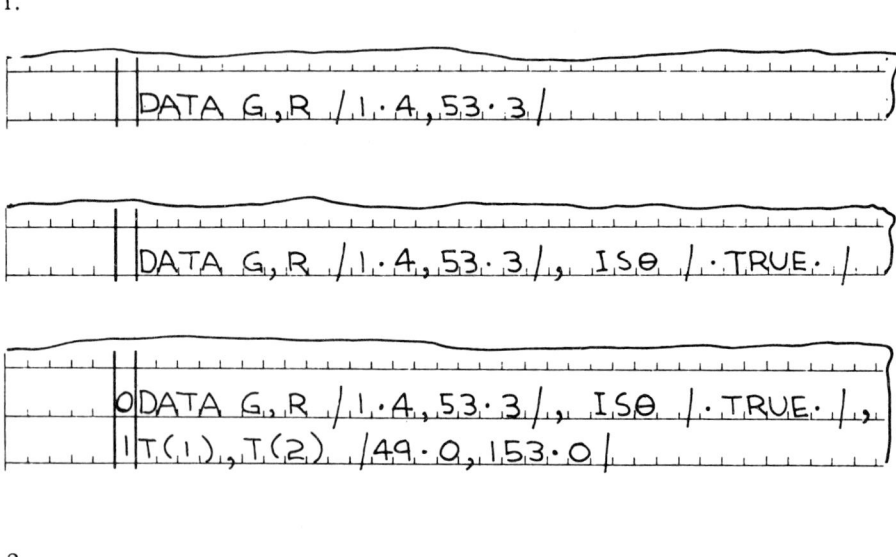

2.

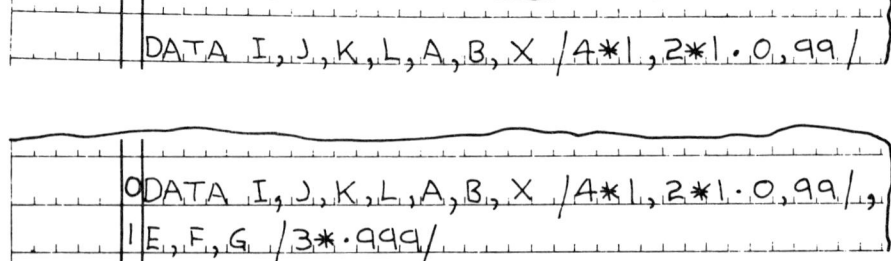

Data Statements can be used to give initial values to any kind of Fortran variable.

Having declared the mode of the variables:

```
LOGICAL Q, A
COMPLEX ARG
DOUBLE PRECISION EXA
```

We could replace the assignment statements:

```
Q, A = .TRUE.
ARG = (1.6, 2.4)
EXA = .312D3
```

by:

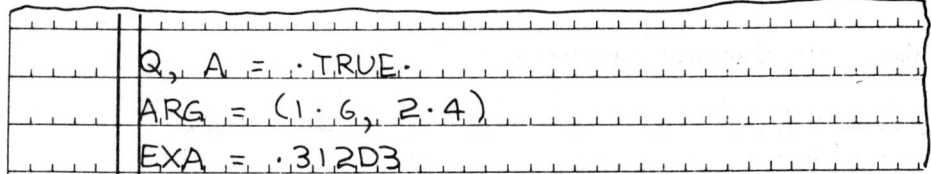

```
ODATA Q,A /2*.TRUE./, ARG/(1.6,2.4)/,
1EXA /.312D3/
```

or of course by:

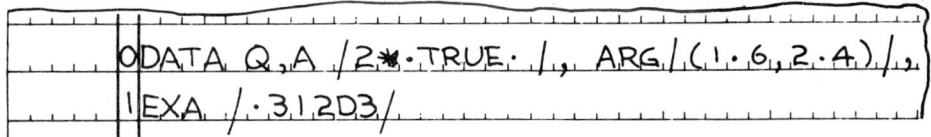

```
ODATA Q,A, ARG, EXA /2*.TRUE.,
1(1.6,2.4), .312D3/
```

337

You can also use the Data Statement to place Text characters in variables.

You will remember that an Integer, Real or Logical variable can hold up to eight characters and Complex and Double Precision sixteen.

To put the eight characters of STARLING into the variable BIRD we write:

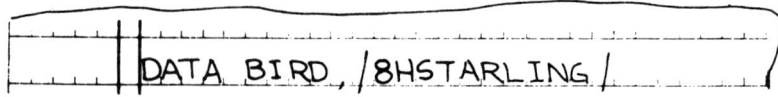

If there are less than eight characters, say:

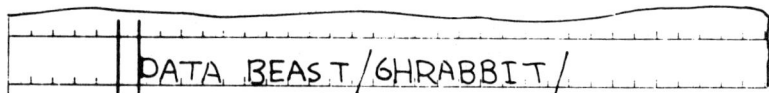

then the remaining rightmost characters will be filled with blanks.

REMINDER

The rule that all the characters, including space characters count in an *H* Format applies here.

338

If the Text data is more than eight characters we can read it into an array.

To read the 21 characters of **PIN-TAILED SANDGROUSE** into the three element array BIRD we would write:

```
DIMENSION BIRD(3)
DATA BIRD(1)/21HPIN-TAILED SANDGROUSE/
```

The first eight characters will be read into BIRD(1) and remaining characters will be read into succeeding elements of the array. Any unused character positions will be filled with blanks.

QUESTION

Make a suitable Dimension Statement and write the Data Statement to put the characters:

WHORTLE-LEAVED WILLOW

in the array:

TREE

ANSWER

```
    | DIMENSION TREE(3)
    | DATA TREE(1) /21HWHORTLE-LEAVED WILLOW/
```

The Block Data Segment

The Block Data Segment is used to give initial values to items in named Common Blocks. Initial values should not be given to items in the Blank Common Block. It is never executed and consequently must contain only non-executable statements.

For example:

Let's say that in a program we have four variables common to both segments:

```
     MASTER ARGO
     REAL MU, K
     COMMON /B1/CP,RHO,MU,K
```

```
     SUBROUTINE CALC
     REAL MU, K
     COMMON /B1/CP,RHO,MU,K
```

We want to give three of the variables initial values:

$$CP = \cdot 1243$$
$$RHO = \cdot 1052$$
$$MU = \cdot 0537$$

343

A program may contain several Block Data Segments each of which starts:

1	2	3	4	5	6	7	8	9	10	11	12	13	14	15	16	17	18	19	20	21	22	23	24	25	26	27	28	29	30	31	32	33	34	35	36	37	38	39
						B	L	O	C	K		D	A	T	A																							

The Common Block must be completely defined. Even variables and array elements which are not to be given initial values must have all the appropriate information stated.

1	2	3	4	5	6	7	8	9	10	11	12	13	14	15	16	17	18	19	20	21	22	23	24	25	26	27	28	29	30	31	32	33	34	35	36	37	38	39
						B	L	O	C	K		D	A	T	A																							
						R	E	A	L		M	U	,		K																							
						C	O	M	M	O	N		/	B	1	/	C	P	,	R	H	O	,	M	U	,	K											

The initial values must of course be given by a Data Statement since it is non-executable

1	2	3	4	5	6	7	8	9	10	11	12	13	14	15	16	17	18	19	20	21	22	23	24	25	26	27	28	29	30	31	32	33	34	35	36	37	38	39
						B	L	O	C	K		D	A	T	A																							
						R	E	A	L		M	U	,		K																							
						C	O	M	M	O	N		/	B	1	/	C	P	,	R	H	O	,	M	U	,	K											
						D	A	T	A		C	P	,	R	H	O	,	M	U	/	.	1	2	4	3	,	.	1	0	5	2	,	.	0	5	3	7	/

and the segment ends with an End Statement.

						E	N	D																														

344

QUESTION

Write a Block Data Segment which will give the following values to the items in Common Blocks:

$$JIK = 3$$
$$NOP = 39$$
$$QUI = \cdot TRUE \cdot$$

1	2	3	4	5	6	7 8 9 10 11 12 13 14 15 16 17 18 19 20 21 22 23 24 25 26 27 28 29 30 31 32 33 34 35 36 37 38
						MASTER PAKE
						LOGICAL QUI, ZEB
						INTEGER SIM
						COMMON /B1/ JIK, SIM, NOP /B2/ QUI, ZEB

1	2	3	4	5	6	7 8 9 10 11 12 13 14 15 16 17 18 19 20 21 22 23 24 25 26 27 28 29 30 31 32 33 34 35 36 37 38
						SUBROUTINE HEW
						LOGICAL QUI, ZEB
						INTEGER SIM
						COMMON /B1/ JIK, SIM, NOP /B2/ QUI, ZEB

ANSWER

C	STATEMENT NUMBER	CONT.	FORTRAN
			BLOCK DATA
			LOGICAL QUI, ZEB
			INTEGER SIM
			COMMON /B1/ JIK, SIM, NOP /B2/ QUI, ZEB
			DATA JIK, NOP /3, 39/, QUI/.TRUE./
			END

Conclusion

To make it easier for you to learn Fortran we've avoided rigorous definitions and have excluded a few of the more advanced features of the language. So, when you start writing Fortran programs in earnest keep the appropriate reference manual to hand until you know the limitations of the particular machine you're programming.

Appendix A

STANDARD FUNCTIONS

TABLE 1 INTRINSIC FUNCTIONS

Intrinsic Function	Definition	Number of Arguments	Symbolic Name	Type of Argument	Type of Function
Absolute Value	$\lvert a \rvert$	1	ABS	REAL	REAL
		1	IABS	INTEGER	INTEGER
		1	DABS	DOUBLE	DOUBLE
Truncation	Sign of a times largest integer $\leqslant \lvert a \rvert$	1	AINT	REAL	REAL
		1	INT	REAL	INTEGER
		1	IDINT	DOUBLE	INTEGER
Nearest Integer	Sign of a times nearest integer $(0 \cdot 5 = 1)$	1	NINT*	REAL	INTEGER
		1	ANINT*	REAL	REAL
Remaindering†	$a_1 \ (\mathrm{mod}\ a_2)$	2	AMOD	REAL	REAL
		2	MOD	INTEGER	INTEGER
Choosing Largest Value	Max $(a_1, a_2, \ldots)$	$\geqslant 2$	AMAX0	INTEGER	REAL
		$\geqslant 2$	AMAX1	REAL	REAL
		$\geqslant 2$	MAX0	INTEGER	INTEGER
		$\geqslant 2$	MAX1	REAL	INTEGER
		$\geqslant 2$	DMAX1	DOUBLE	DOUBLE
Choosing Smallest Value	Min $(a_1, a_2, \ldots)$	$\geqslant 2$	AMIN0	INTEGER	REAL
		$\geqslant 2$	AMIN1	REAL	REAL
		$\geqslant 2$	MIN0	INTEGER	INTEGER
		$\geqslant 2$	MIN1	REAL	INTEGER
		$\geqslant 2$	DMIN1	DOUBLE	DOUBLE
Float	Conversion from integer to real	1	FLOAT	INTEGER	REAL
Fix	Conversion from real to integer	1	IFIX	REAL	INTEGER
Transfer of Sign	Sign of a_2 times $\lvert a_1 \rvert$	2	SIGN	REAL	REAL
		2	ISIGN	INTEGER	INTEGER
		2	DSIGN	DOUBLE	DOUBLE

* Indicates available in 1900 FORTRAN but not necessarily available in standard FORTRAN.

† The function MOD or AMOD (a_1, a_2) is defined as $a_1 - [a_1/a_2]a_2$, where $[x]$ is the largest integer whose magnitude does not exceed the magnitude of x and whose sign is the same as x.

TABLE 1—*contd.*

Intrinsic Function	Definition	Number of Arguments	Symbolic Name	Type of	
				Argument	Function
Positive Difference	$a_1 - \text{Min } (a_1, a_2)$	2	DIM	REAL	REAL
		2	IDIM	INTEGER	INTEGER
Obtain Most Significant Part of Double Precision Argument		1	SNGL	DOUBLE	REAL
Obtain Real Part of Complex Argument		1	REAL	COMPLEX	REAL
Obtain Imaginary Part of Complex Argument		1	AIMAG	COMPLEX	REAL
Express Single Precision Argument in Double Precision Form		1	DBLE	REAL	DOUBLE
Express Two Real Arguments in Complex Form	$a_1 + a_2 \sqrt{-1}$	2	CMPLX	REAL	COMPLEX
Obtain Conjugate of a Complex Argument		1	CONJG	COMPLEX	COMPLEX

TABLE 2 BASIC EXTERNAL FUNCTIONS

Basic External Function	Definition	Number of Arguments	Symbolic Name	Type of	
				Argument	Function
Exponential	e^a	1	EXP	REAL	REAL
		1	DEXP	DOUBLE	DOUBLE
		1	CEXP	COMPLEX	COMPLEX
Exponential to base 10	10^a	1	EXP10*	REAL	REAL
Natural Logarithm	$\log_e (a)$	1	ALOG	REAL	REAL
		1	DLOG	DOUBLE	DOUBLE
		1	CLOG	COMPLEX	COMPLEX
Common Logarithm	$\log_{10} (a)$	1	ALOG10	REAL	REAL
		1	DLOG10	DOUBLE	DOUBLE
Base 2 Logarithm	$\log_2 (a)$	1	ALOG2*	REAL	REAL
Trigonometric Sine (radians)	$\sin (a)$	1	SIN	REAL	REAL
		1	DSIN	DOUBLE	DOUBLE
		1	CSIN	COMPLEX	COMPLEX
Trigonometric Cosine (radians)	$\cos (a)$	1	COS	REAL	REAL
		1	DCOS	DOUBLE	DOUBLE
		1	CCOS	COMPLEX	COMPLEX
Trigonometric Tangent (radians)	$\tan (a)$	1	TAN*	REAL	REAL
Trigonometric Cotangent (radians)	$\cot (a)$	1	COT*	REAL	REAL
Hyperbolic Sine	$\sinh (a)$	1	SINH*	REAL	REAL
Hyperbolic Cosine	$\cosh (a)$	1	COSH*	REAL	REAL
Hyperbolic Tangent	$\tanh (a)$	1	TANH	REAL	REAL
Hyperbolic Cotangent	$\coth (a)$	1	COTH*	REAL	REAL
Square Root	$(a)^{1/2}$	1	SQRT	REAL	REAL
		1	DSQRT	DOUBLE	DOUBLE
		1	CSQRT	COMPLEX	COMPLEX
Arcsine	$\sin^{-1} (a)$	1	ASIN*	REAL	REAL
Arc-cosine	$\cos^{-1} (a)$	1	ACOS*	REAL	REAL

* Indicates available in 1900 FORTRAN but not necessarily available in standard FORTRAN.

350

TABLE 2—*contd.*

Basic External Function	Definition	Number of Arguments	Symbolic Name	Type of	
				Argument	Function
Arctangent	$\tan^{-1}(a)$	1	ATAN	REAL.	REAL
		1	DATAN	DOUBLE	DOUBLE
(angles in radians)	$\tan^{-1}(a_1/a_2)$	2	ATAN2	REAL	REAL
		2	DATAN2	DOUBLE	DOUBLE
Arc-cotangent	$\cot^{-1}(a)$	1	ACOT*	REAL	REAL
Inverse Hyperbolic Sine	$\sinh^{-1}(a)$	1	ASINH*	REAL	REAL
Inverse Hyperbolic Cosine	$\cosh^{-1}(a)$	1	ACOSH*	REAL	REAL
Inverse Hyperbolic Tangent	$\tanh^{-1}(a)$	1	ATANH*	REAL	REAL
Inverse Hyperbolic Cotangent	$\coth^{-1}(a)$	1	ACOTH*	REAL	REAL
Remaindering†	$a_1 \pmod{a_2}$	2	DMOD	DOUBLE	DOUBLE
Modulus		1	CABS	COMPLEX	REAL

* Indicates available in 1900 FORTRAN but not necessarily available in standard FORTRAN.

† The function DMOD (a_1, a_2) is defined as $a_1 - [a_1/a_2]a_2$, where $[x]$ is the largest integer whose magnitude does not exceed the magnitude of x and whose sign is the same as the sign of x.

The only significant difference between the two sets of standard functions is that the Intrinsic functions cannot appear in EXTERNAL statements and cannot be actual arguments of subroutines or functions.

Appendix B

You are restricted to the following characters in Fortran:

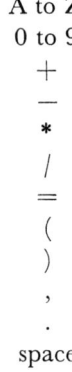

A to Z
0 to 9
+
—
*
/
=
(
)
,
.
space

After an H Format you can use any of the characters in the machine's character set.

Index